How I became a bandit

by

Carmine Crocco

CARMINE CROCCO

Edited and translated by

Barbara Luciana Di fiore

Carmine Crocco

CARMINE CROCCO

CHAPTER ONE – THE CHILDHOOD

On the 27th of March 1889 in St. Stefano's bathroom, where I serve my term of imprisonment, I begin to write my memories; by reading this test, do not expect things that make the human soul be joyful, but rather that make him feel sad and horrified.

My country, called Rionero in Vulture, is located in the district of Melfi, in Basilicata, Italy, and is on the slope of a hill to the east of a mountain named Monticchio. The entire territory is covered with vineyards, olive groves, vegetables, chestnut trees, fields, forests and pastures, full of wonderful vegetation. According to some people, its population is made of 12,000 inhabitants among those there is the real Lucania prototype, mentioned by Telemachus. To the south of this beautiful country, set a few meters away from the body of the country itself, there are about twenty houses of a single floor, placed along the slope of a bank whose height varies between 25 and 50 meters. Each of these houses was inhabited by a family of poor farmers and cultivators, who working hard kept misery and hunger away. However, among those people there were the shoemaker, who was a secret spy of the Bourbon police, the stone-cutter, some decurions, the gossip, the tailor and the school teacher, for those who could pay for him.

Those families were formed by 200 inhabitants, more or less; if we add to these people a hundred animals, among those there were sheeps, goats, oxes, pigs and donkeys, which are part of the poor, we will have the amount of five hundred animated beings, all inhabitants of those smoked hovels.

Yet, in that place there were glorious, old and mutilated veterans of Napoleon, covered with wounds that they had got in Spain, Prussia, Austria, and against the Cossacks of the priest; there were a lot of men who had endured the Bourbon, Republican, Murattian, Bonapartist turpitudes and other misfortunes. There were respectable old ladies, who were still virgin and had not given in to the French, Jacobin and Spanish filths, during the fishy days when men protected themselves thanks to their own strengths, since governments, while waiting for fighting against each other, shot helpless men as they need their blood, imprisoned innocent people as they need money, as they need revenge. In the long winter evenings, those old men told each other the wonderful stories of their turbulent lives, of the battles they won, of the valuable actions they had made, of the blood that flowed along the battlefields full of dead and wounded people, which toughened our souls because of our warlike and bellicose nature.

In one of those houses that I mentioned above, the first Sunday of June 1830 I was born from Francesco Crocco Donatelli and Maria Gera from Santo Mauro.

My mother married in 1824 and from this year up to 1836 when I began to remember events, my mother gave birth to five children, named Donato, Carmine, who is me, Rosina, Antonio, and Marco; the sixth was to come into the world, but God was envious of our happiness and began to scourge us. Now I want to tell about the happiness of a poor family.

My father was a shepherd and a farmer; when he married his wife, he went away from his father, bought a few sheeps and a few goats, and after depriving a noble family of a piece of land which they had rent, he began to sow wheat, legumes, formentone and a little hemp. Thanks to his daily work he earned enough money to pay the rent to the owner and provide for the survival of the family, while thanks to the sheeps and the goats he earned other money in order to pay for the household expenses. My mother had inherited a mound of land, where vineyards were planted, and they were our delight; she had also two little houses and was a wool worker, thanks to which she was able to feed her family.

Both my father and my mother, God has called them to peace, gave us everything. It was nice in the morning when my father opened the fold and the goats came outside, hopping along the grazing areas, while we all, as kids, ran together and raced with each other looking for flowers to bring to our mother.

And my mother had a lot of goodness in his eyes full of love, a lot of love in its behavior full of care, a lot of constant willingness to work! He got up at dawn, prepared her husband's saddlebag, tidied her house, took care of her children, and with a lot of energy she began to work, sure to earn her 40 cents before sunset.

How much patience a mother should have in raising her children! A baby cries, screams as much as they can do and the mother does her best to calm them, and she often does not succeed in doing it. She feeds them and they say no; she gives them a piece of bread, and they throw it away; she gives them a toy and they break it; she puts them down on the floor and they roll in the mud; she puts them into the cradle and they jump off, and the mother is full of patience, kisses them and covers them with love. Yet, I met some men who said,"They are just women and nothing else!", how much contempt for women. Shut up male: women are the mothers of men, women are the wifes of men, there is no life without them. Women are the daughters of men, there are no happy fathers without them; and finally women are the sisters of men, there are no happy brothers without them, neither a happy family.

Think about what Guerazzi wrote: "you must respect the woman because her mother was so" and if you do not deeply feel this respect in yourself, grasp the plow and hoe the ground, you do not deserve a better fate.

I felt a so powerful and a so strong affection for my mother, that in those moments when my desire was at his maximum level his memory acted as a stimulus, and she appeared before my eyes with her proud look, staring strongly at my face, as if to say "Hit, lay claim to me, the others did not feel pity for me, for your father and for your sister."

And now after so many years I repeat that a child who has the luck to be born from a virtuous mother, if she receives the slightest insult from an overbearing man and does not take revenge, her child is a coward, an insignificant man. So when I was born and I believed that I had a role in this world, because of an outrage to my poor mother, I worked hard to kill a lot of people and I marvelously managed to do that!

Forgive the outburst of a sorrowful soul, my dear reader, and be polite with me, agree with me and let's go to my place. You will not find sofas, dressers, tables, chairs and other objects, there is nothing luxurious or comfortable. These are two small houses blackened by the passing of the time and by the smoke; one of them is used as a barn and a stable for the animals, in the other one we sleep. Can you see that miserable bed supported by rotten beams and rusted trestles? My father and my mother sleep there; in the near little bed we, three siblings, sleep, all in swaddling bands as stockfishes. Can you see in the big basket? There, our little sister sleeps; and in the cradle, suspended on the bed and manufactured with a few wicker and straw, Marco, the last born, come into the world just a few months ago, sleeps. Here is my mother who works with the wool, can you see her? She is totally stained with oil. Look at that smoked chest, it contains pumpernickel, formentone, broad beans, peas and little grain with which we could make white bread when God punishes us with diseases. It is the harvest done by my father, God knows how much sweat he poured for a few legumes! Raise your eyes to the ceiling, can you see how blackened are those beams because of the smoke and the walls full of soot? Can you feel the smell of goats, sheeps, rabbits, chickens? What do you say about it? On the window sill of a fake window there are the kitchen utensils, pots, pans and dishes made of clay, wooden spoons, a copper pot, that's all. I take advantage of your goodness and I invite you to sit on these wooden seats, made with an ax by my father, so I will have the pleasure to introduce you to my uncle Martino, my school teacher. He is an old first gunnery sergeant and during the siege of Saragossa in Spain he lost his left leg carried away by a cannon ball; he was born here. There is another old man who had his arm cut off by a Uhlan and now that poor man lives by begging, because the Bourbon government has not recognized the poor pension he had from Gioacchino Murat.

Further, there is another old blind man; he lost his sight in Berezina, and now he lives singing verbum caro. But you came here to know other sort of things and not to hear about a lame, a mutilated and a blind. But I want to conclude that the governments, generally speaking, never look at where children of poverty were born, nor how they make a living, and they do not anything to mitigate their poverty in some ways and remove their ignorance. Instead they look for them when they are all men able to live by themselves and to give some relief to their older parents. So the governor, without forgetting one of them, take them all as they were his property and he does what he pleases with them.

The pretext is beautiful, the Homeland, the Law, the first is a whore, the second is even worse.

And the Homeland and the Law have rights and duties, and want the blood of the children of poverty. But is there a law that is equal for everyone? Do not tell me that, do not to talk about this tremendous giant, because I know that the fair law never existed nor will exist as long as God will not exterminate us all. My innocent father did not find neither the law nor the justice; instead Don Vincenzo C. found it, he was the murderer of my mother. As for me, I do not hate neither the law nor the government, I owe them my life, but then I repeat again what Mastrogianni and Victor Hugo wrote: "Let him live in misery and infamy!".

And here I am to the reasons why there was the spark that from 1860 to 1864 caused so much blood in Puglia and Basilicata.

We are in 1836. One morning in April, Donato, my older brother and I were back from our uncle Martino's school. A few minutes after entering home Donato was sent to collect the grass for the rabbits and I went to buy some salt to cook. We ran as fast as rats do, one of us to the east and the other to the west and fifteen minutes later we were back; each having done their own duty very well, there was no beating, since when we made the slightest mistake there were slaps and clouts. To me my mother's beatings were so tasty that I sometimes made mistakes on purpose to have them. It was lunch time and we sat around a table with a large bowl of steaming soup on it, we began to eat, while my mother gave milk to her little son. This group, which was happy even if it was poor, made Satan so envious, that he wanted to destroy them, and forever; in another corner of the room there was another group of happy animals, rabbits and chickens eating the grass collected by Donato, and the Devil, perhaps even jealous of the beasts, wanted to disturb that happiness; indeed he used those beasts to bring misfortune into our house.

Unexpectedly, a beautiful greyhound dog came into our room with a jump and after grabbing a rabbit ran outside. After seeing what had happened we all began to scream and went outside to make the animal leave its prey. It disturbed our joy, but unfortunately the rabbit was dead. Donato, who was going to pick up a cudgel, hit with a tremendous blow the dog's head, and the magnificent greyhound fell down dead on the spot. Unhappily, that dog belonged to a rich man, named Vincenzo C... who after noticing that his dog wasn't near there, turned back and as he found it dead near our house, addressed a million of insults to my mother's place, and began to beat us with his whip. My mother tried to apologize, to beg pardon, to beg for pity, but it was all a wasting of breath, and the man, absolutely wanting to know who had killed his dog, went on punching the poor Donato, holding him by his arm. Then my mother after seeing his son being scourged, did her best to protect him; she put her little son, who was in her arms, on the ground and rushed furiously towards the man, but he was really mad and vigorously kicked her into her belly, which made her fall to the ground half dead.

The brutal man, after committing the crime and having given vent to his infamous anger, cried as the vilest of human beings could do. Don Vincenzo did so.

After having nearly killed a 5-month-pregnant woman, he locked himself in his room, and began to cry. He cried not for fear of the law, for fear of the justice, of a sentence, that certainly would have been given to the poor like us; he knew very well that the justice lives millions and millions of meters away from the houses of the rich and the powerful, but he cried for the shame and the remorse. The frightened relatives rushed over, a doctor arrived, but my mother did not recover consciousness; God chose to let her open her eyes. But it would have been better for her if she had never opened them!

From April 1836 to May 1839 the poor woman was forced to stay in bed. Who can say how much we cried, the oldest of us was eight years old, the youngest was only two! Who would have thought about us? Who would have washed us, combed our hair, tidied clothes? Who would have stroked us? Oh, how often I craved my mother loving slaps!

My father could not leave his job, we would have died of hunger. Our aunt was a thief and a glutton but she began to take care of the house; she stole everything she found before her eyes, devoured everything was good, leaving the bad and smelly food to us. Goodbye schools, goodbye uncle Martino, relatives, classmates, friends, goodbye everyone!

Despair and misery are with us. Death and prison are there for the miserable!

Yet, we have a Master overhead, God, a man on the earth, the King. In that period our King was Francesco II and our Queen was Maria Cristina; the Neapolitans' holy and good King; but they only took care of parties and glory, while we were dying of hunger.

After a strenuous abortion my mother seemed to improve, it was then that my father went to Venosa, under the Santangelo lords' control to shear the sheeps and to harvest wheat.

In the meanwhile, Don Vincenzo C., the murderer of my mother, locked in his palace, had thought to the danger of a revenge and, wisely, had managed to make my father leave his role as a local guard, in consequence of which he had to abandon his rifle.

But God always punishes people; one morning Don Vincenzo, alone, went to the countryside on a superb black horse. He was armed like an old knight; he had some guns attached to the saddle, a rifle to the bandolier and a dagger. But, in spite of all this stuff, before he could get to the area called La Torre, about three miles far from Rionero, he was shot, which made him fall to the ground bleeding. Another man was watching over him and, informed of that trip by a spy, after measuring the time and the place, gave vent to his hatred, almost certain of his impunity, as he knew that he would not have been accused of the unsuccessful murder, because he would have infamously blamed on another man, thanks to contemptible and misleading statements.

Unfortunately, the hand of the coward was trembling, maybe not for the murder he was about to make, but for the false accusation with which he blamed on an innocent person; and so it was that Don Vincenzo C. was touched lightly by the bullet and lost a strand of hair.

The attempted assassination of Don Vincenzo had to be punished even if it would have caused innocent victims; it was necessary to give the guilty to the justice, or at least make some arrests, actually many arrests, to show that Del Carretto General's men do not stay there without doing anything. Who do you think was the first person arrested?

Right, my father, my own father, who was in Venosa when the crime was committed, in Don Felice Santangelo's house, nine miles far from Rionero. The statements of his masters in Venosa were useless and the statements of twenty-eight honest people who worked with my father were so, as well. The crime was so obvious, so natural, that no statement could destroy the belief that he was the murderer, therefore, Francesco Donatelli, sent to jail, was subjected to a criminal prosecution.

Five other poor men, responsible for feeding their families, were arrested, as well. The police had found some reasons why they could have committed the crime against Don Vincenzo. According to these reasons they would have had to arrest more people, as the squire's arrogance was so excessive that he had argued with all the local farmers for numerous reasons, for transit reasons, for waters origin reasons, for rent payments reasons, for harvest division reasons, and so on.

Those strict judges fantasizing about the crime causes did not remember the famous saying "Cherchez la femme!" The instigator had been a woman, one of Don Vincenzo's friends. How many tears for that filthy woman!

Who can consider the pain of an innocent man in prison, with the danger of falling into the executioner's hands. The offender does not suffer as his conscience is quiet and we could say: I am guilty and I suffer for a punishment that I deserve; but the innocent never rests, the innocent does not know how to regain his lost liberty, suffers for the infamy that covers his name, and he cries, curses, dams... but in vain.

My father imprisonment had a repercussion on my mother's bad health. When the poor woman heard of her husband arrest was petrified, she refused to eat and soon went crazy. One day she cried, the day after she laughed, the following day she threw herself off the bed, tried to go out on the street wearing just her nightdress and destroyed everything she found before her eyes, and if we tried to get close to her, she threatened to strangle us. The only person who could get close to her and influence her was her brother, who had a lot of children and had to think of hoeing the ground to feed his family instead of taking care of his sister.

My father wrote agonizing letters from the prison in Potenza, and heartily recommended his relatives, friends, wife and children, but in the meantime our little heritage was about to finish and in a few days we became very poor.

Our uncle, our mother's brother, made all our relatives gather together, and it was decided that his sister Rosina would have gone with her maternal aunt. Antonio went to a paternal uncle' place and died shortly afterwards, burned alive; Marco, the youngest, went under the thief aunt control who during our poor mother's illness stole everything. Donato went to pasture the sheeps at a gentleman's house, and I did the same but at another lord's house in Puglia.

I was far from my country, far from my crazy mother, far from my father who was in prison and I grew up putting out the sheeps to pasture, I grew up with the poison in my heart, with the anger in my soul, with the strong desire to hurt people. One day, after a long time, I was told to go to Rionero to try an experiment in order to make my mother regain consciousness. When I entered the house and saw my mother who resembled a skeleton, I ran to hug her, but she pushed me away in horror and said, "Carry this snake far from me."

Oh merciful God, my mother knew that I was the venomous snake, which had to bite my fellows, which had to poison many families, I had to be transformed into a nasty reptile! If I had considered that prophecy, if I had just meditated on my mother's rejection, maybe I would not have soiled my hands with so much blood. Actually, what I said is not true; it was because of my mother's misfortunes that I became a killer, those misfortunes made me inhuman, sometimes ferocious; and when I killed those who asked for pity, I was so cruel right because of the pains my mother had suffered from.

But now thinking about the past is useless, I had to become a killer, and so I did! I had not come back to Puglia, and in spite of my mother's rejections towards me, the doctor hoped to succeed in something with the poor crazy woman using my person, when one day I heard the bell of the parish with gloomy tolls which was a call to bring all the people together for one of their countrymen's funeral. Francesco A., called uncle Cecco, was dead.

"Poor dead, what a pity! What do you want, after all, he was old, may God grant him peace. He confessed and died as a saint. Tomorrow he will have a sung mass and his coffin, he will have the lighting, two offices and the participation of all the brothers belonging to the Saint Sacrament congregation, may he rest in peace..." these were the people's talks.

In fact, the church had been prepared for a funeral, the altar had been covered with candles, the coffin had been covered with silk and gold drapes, and everyone had gathered to take part in uncle Cecco's funeral, a venerable good man. And he was really a good man, poor dead. When there were misfortunes he was the first to help, he begged and scolded those who made mistakes; he was jealous of the others' honor, as he was of his honor, he advised people to do well. I remember his countenance very well, in spite of the passing of the years. He was quite high, he had a broad forehead, big and black eyes, a wide chest, muscular arms and legs, a long, white and shabby beard that gave him a wild look.

The church was crowded with people, the women sobbed beating themselves on the chest, the men were silent and sad, only Don Leonardo Cecero, prior of the parish, looked troubled.

When the mass began, under the sound of a funeral music, after the elevation, Don Leonardo, told the masses that he wanted to speak. Everyone believed that the respectable pastor magnify uncle Cecero's many virtues, so there was soon a sepulchral silence. Don Leonardo said something like that: "Gentlemen, people, men and women, you all knew Francesco A. Before his death he left five thousand liras to enlarge the church and a thousand of liras for the poor and the indigent of the parish. In addition, he gave me this document begging me to read it in your presence.

"Not all of you can understand the importance of this document in which there are abundant quotations in Latin and Greek, so I will tell you the most important part.

"When there was the Neapolitan Republic, Francesco killed five people living in Mandorano and destroyed their houses, when there was Giuseppe Bonaparte, King of the Two Sicilies, he killed a French because he was jelous of some bad women. In 1809, he slaughtered King Gioacchino Murat special commissioner in one of his wives' place. He killed the forester Michele Spiarule, and recently, tried to kill Don Vincenzo C.

"Our uncle Cecco tried to go on with this unsuccessful murder to revenge Margherita, a foundling grown up in his place, seduced by D. Vincenzo and obliged to go to a brothel."

Leonardo invoked the blessing of heaven on the body of the departed, encouraged the faithful to pray for his soul, asked for his forgiveness, to the children and the grandchildren of those who were killed by him and promised that he would soon made King Ferdinando II know all the events, in order to obtain the release of the innocent accused of D. Vincenzo C.'s murder.

So my father was innocent, and his innocence was proclaimed loudly and clearly to everyone. Uncle Cecco did not want to bring the secret of his crimes in his grave. He could have left a good memory of himself, because no one knew that he was guilty, he preferred to get rid of his soul's remorse; and in my opinion he did well, since he partly amended for his serious sins. I know a lot of people who think or thought about that in a different way, who were, during their life, rich and respectable, and when they died had the honor of a long lasting memory although they were guilty and sad. I know people who, after the collapse of the Bourbon power, were the heads of the repression, had thousands and thousands of shields in their hands, and secretly began practicing with me and my group in order to raise the masses, and afterwards pretending to be liberals, betrayed Francesco II as they had first betrayed Vittorio Emanuele. And since I do not want to blame them, and to give their children or grandchildren those damned souls, I have to die without confessing, even if I could get some people's close relatives blush with shame, with one single word! But I do not want to alarm the guilty and their relatives, I will not speak; their names will die with me.

The priest Don Leonardo Cecero as a true minister of God does, kept his promise, he was in Naples, talked to Ferdinando II, and my father was released soon. But his freedom was conditioned. After a 31-month-imprisonment, guilty of being a victim's relative of a gentleman, he began to be observed by the police. And my father decided to surrender and did not want to rebel. Oh wife! oh children! you are the ones who have the power of making the man feel not free to choose what to do.

But it was different for me! I was growing up with hatred in the heart; my body was becoming bigger and a lively desire to avenge all the pains my mother and my father had suffered from was becoming bigger, as well.

When I was 15 I felt I was an adult; I was not afraid of anyone, and I felt the need to prevail on my peers, to stand out from the average man, even if it was dangerous for my life.

House of Carmine Crocco

CHAPTER TWO - THE FIRST MURDER

In 1845 I rescued Giovanni Aquilecchia from Atella from the Ofanto waters; he was a wealthy person, who gave me 50 shields for my action.

That sum represented a treasure for me, accustomed to earn two pounds a month; I thought I was rich, therefore after saying goodbye to my sheeps, and to the fertile level grounds in Puglia I decided to leave for Rionero. I had been away from home for over 5 years, I had so many thoughts in my soul and the memory of my dear parents had a powerful attraction for me.

My father had influenced me a lot, but I could not understand why although he had been so strong and vigorous, he had decided to give in to the social injustices and had quietly accepted all the cruelest insults by so many people. Frankly speaking, my predominant idea was that of influencing my father's soul, of encouraging him to abandon his role as a slave. Now, I would remove everyone from the humble condition of being shepherds and encourage them to take their chances. The work did not make me feel afraid, I felt healthy and well, I was accustomed to hardships, and I would gladly have worked hard all day long if I could have cultivated my piece of land

But unfortunately I was not born to hoe the ground, I could not have the happiness of an honest man; the crazy lady's snake had to act as a disgusting reptile does and poison her life and those belonging to thousands of people. And unfortunately, things went on in this way.

And now that, alone in this prison, I think of my past and try to find out the reason why I was born in misery, but I have had respectable and honest ideas since my childhood and I could not give up, with the passing of the time, this immense desire to prevail, to become even a big villain, I realize that there are different reasons.

The first and most important thing was those few things that Uncle Martin was able to teach me with religious patience. And as in the kingdom of the blind this kind of men are considered as gentlemen, this way I felt totally superior to those around me, who were coarse and illiterate, while I was able able to write letters and poems.

The nomadic life I had when I was a child and a guardian of the horses, helped me to develop the seeds of greatness. By taking part into fairs I visited Bari, Barletta, Andria, Altamura, Foggia, Gravina, Cerignola, so I learned that the world and the life was not enclosed within the Vulture boundaries and the Monticchio woods.

By purchasing agreements stipulated every day I saw a lot of money, and my masters managed to increase their heritage that was already very large, without working, rather sitting in the shade of their villas; and I thought about the reason why they were so lucky and we were so poor, although we were the ones who worked very hard. In addition, we had to be subjected to many misfortunes, therefore, it is not difficult to imagine the reason why, with the passing of the time, I became so famous, not for my values and my good actions, but for my infamy and my evil deeds. My father did not listen to my proposals; he showed me that he was happy in spite of his misery, he tried to calm down my feeling of magnitude and advised me to keep on being humble and hardworking.

I left him to his farm or rather to this master's farm, and by mutual agreement we decided that I would be back in Rionero to look for a job and my sister Rosina would have come with me. There I lived happily for a little, working a land belonging to Don Biagio Lo Vaglio. He was a good and charitable man and in his house there were many families of farmers, who knew about the misfortunes of my family and were very kind and generous with me. The farmer, Marco Consiglio gave me a part of a land, the number 85, a pair of oxes, the stable number 5, the plow and the working tools, and considered me as a son.

Later, thanks to my will and my hard work I became good at the art of agriculture, and I could devote myself to cultivate my part of land. In the first year the harvest was good and fertile and God rewarded my sweat. Wheat, peas, chickpeas, beans, potatoes, pumpkins and tomatoes were so abundant that I did not know where to put them. Oh land, fertile mother! So God created Adamo told him to become a farmer not a King!

After doing the harvest, paying the rent and the oxes toll, I realized that I had earned two liras per day, while at first, when I was at the second master's farm, I received 36 cents and I had to work three times more and, worse than that, I was a slave night and day. I was happy and content and my sister Rosina was happier than me and was a little housewife keeping the house perfectly tidy.

In the evening we gathered with several families in a stable to listen to the stories the old men told us. I remember a nice gay who was about seventy, still healthy and strong, who only knew how to write his name and wanted to be considered as a scientist, and he got angry if we opposed him. He told us of the republican period, and stated that he had taken part in the fall of Vienna, in the conquest of Berlin, in the battle of Jena, and in the retreat from Moscow. He had a strong memory and mentioned historical events that had occurred under Giuseppe Buonaparte's and Gioacchino Murat's governments, as well as those happened when there was the Cardinal Ruffo. After the story of commissions by several band leaders, like Vandarelli from Foggia or Fra Diavolo from Itri, or Talarico or Taccone, that old and wise man taught us a lot of things saying, "My dear children, always try to be good, with the law, with your superiors, with your masters; run away from bad companions, do good actions when you can, and by doing so you will enjoy freedom and respect and you will always be good men, and despite being poor, if you will behave honestly, your life will go on and God will provide for everything. My dear children, I am happier to eat acorns cooked under the ashes, rather than chickens and capons that have been stolen, and I can swear that a pug earned working hard is better than a hundred thousand ducats that have been stolen."

Poor old man, he could never assume that the person who was close to him, and occasionally offered him to drink, was precisely like Fra Diavolo and Vandarelli! And for more than one evening I listened to those paternal advice and to the refrain that the old man kept on repeating: "Do good things and you will receive good things."

Thanks to those stories I learned to distinguish the good from the evil; as long as I received the good I was good, too, but when I was hurt by the evil, I became poisonous as a monstrous snake.

You do not have to believe, however, that Carmine Donatelli Crocco was really a thief and a murderer, or a bad person, as someone thinks; nothing of these things. I used my cruelty to protect myself and, since I had a strong body, quick reflexes, an acute understanding and fast movements, when my opponent gave me a second, I was able to kill him, even if he had a gun or stones. Moreover, since I was a lover of peace, tranquility, obedience, respect to my superiors, to the law and I was ready to help my fellows, I did not look for quarrels, but if anyone teased me, they would have been in trouble. I have been subjected to a lot of pains for 25 years, I've never quarreled with anyone and I put an end to hundreds of fights that without me would have transformed into deaths.

But I want to come back to my story and to my early years. One morning in May 1847 I was plowing the land in Mr. Lo Vaglio's farm, when a young man born in a noble family, sat on a superb horse and accompanied by a dozen hounds, passed near me. I stopped the plow, rested for a while and stared at the young man who was coming towards me; my workmate, seeing that I was resting,, passed near me and said, "Hurry up young man, the night is coming down, do not look at the son of the infamous Don Vincenzo C. .., you may have a misfortune, even if people say that he is not like his brutal and evil father."

"Dear Uncle Matteo, I said, I am waiting for him to teach him a lesson, and if he is not satisfied, I will give him a second one, but it will be excessive." That young man, as you well remember, dear reader, was the son of the murderer of my mother; so you can imagine my feelings at the time. When it was within my reach, I went towards him and with a hoarse voice exclaimed, "Man, tell your dogs to go back, otherwise ... "; with this phrase I was hoping to get him angry, to have a quarrel with him and to kill him, but God did not want this to happen. The young patrician stopped his horse, dismounted and summoned his dogs, then he came toward me and greeted me asking me why I had told him to summon his dogs, and if they were disturbing me.

"Surely Mr. Don Ferdinandino, I said, the wheat is in bloom, and if a dog steps on it, it breaks the tender stalk and the spike is lost, which is a loss for us, because the owner does not want to know about damages and we have to pay for them."

"I assure you that I did not know about it, he said, and I thank you for the lesson, what is your name, young man? '.

"I'm Carmine Donatelli Crocco, I'm here to serve your lordship."

The squire mounted his horse and went away at full gallop; in the evening Vito De Feo, a sheep manager working at La Torre's farm came to see me, begging me to come to Ferdinandino C.'s place because he wanted to talk to me. I did not want they could suppose I was afraid, so I put on my jacket, I made sure that I had a knife and went to La Torre, accompanied by Vito. I was received like a respectable man, I was given a glass of liqueur, some cookies from France, an Havana cigar and I was invited to sit on a comfortable chair.

Don Ferdinando talked about my family's misfortunes making me several questions; in reply I showed him a manuscript where there was the story of our misfortunes. The man read it and not annoyed said:

"Yesterday did you try to provoke me?".

"If yesterday your lordship had used his whip as your father used to do, I said, I would have shot you; after I would have taken your horse, I would have gone to my father, and I would have done justice against all those witnesses who had told lies about my father."

The man spoke a lot, he said that the sins of the fathers should not relapse into their children; assured me that it was willing to help all of his father's victims, starting with my family, and asked me if I wanted to become his farm's farmer.

I thanked him and declined his offer, being happy with my three mounds of land, thanks to which I hoped to earn two hundred crowns which I needed to absolve my military service. The man really wanted to give me a gift for the service exemption, but I refused and asked him to give me what I would have missed at the time of my military service. So we made an agreement and I went back home full of enthusiasm for Don Ferdinandino who was hopeful for me. But fate was against me.

The young nobleman being embroiled in political parties, during the revolution of May 15th 1848, in Naples, was massacred by the Swiss mercenaries under the palace belonging to the Duke of Gravina, and as I did not have his support, and consequently the two hundred ecus, I had to become a soldier.

And here I am, a soldier of Ferdinando II; I left from Potenza in March 19th 1849 and I arrived in Naples on the 26th, admitted to the first regiment of artillery. On June 24th, I joined my group in Palermo. I liked the military service, and it did not seem heavy to me; what I hated was to see almost every day my companions being beaten, because they did not pay enough attention and sometimes lacked of discipline. As for me, accustomed to the strong features of the men from Puglia, the rigid and strict discipline did not frighten me. At first I cried thinking of my country, my friends, my girlfriend (who immediately forgot about me marrying another man, that I turned into a bandit); but little by little I got used to it and I became an excellent soldier with a rare conduct, as shown by the serial numbers of the second company of the first Artillery Regiment.

On December 16th, 1851 I set off from Palermo and on the 18th I arrived in Gaeta to meet my new garrison, where I was, better being less far from my friends. In the meanwhile, my sister had celebrated her 18th birthday. Her height was normal, she was slim, her head was covered by a mass of blond hair, her chin was oval, her eyes black, her nose and mouth of the right size, her face was round, her breast was large and pompous. The poor girl was living without a father or a mother, who were very far from her, she had been separated from her brother, a soldier, and earned a living working 14 hours a day, and was happy in her misery. She was proud and her loving nature had not been indifferent to the love one of the peasants of the area felt for her. He occasionally sang: " Dove which jumps and reaches my arms …" But one day an infamous woman, a procuress, called Rosa with her mock hypocrisy and false affection tried to enter the young shepherdess' virgin soul and, when she thought it was right, encouraged her to meet a gentleman called Don Peppino C. Her answer was a wound in the lady's face, which she deserved a lot. The lady hid her wound and my sister ran into her house asking for their parents' protection and help. After the occurrence of these things, I received a letter from Rionero where I found out what had happened.

Honest people can imagine the way I was feeling reading that letter, I almost felt a storm in my heart. A dishonest man had dragged us into misery and despair, another man with the same features, belonging to an infamous family (since each one of the six brothers had their own girlfriend, and their mother was aware of that, actually she had acted as a procuress) wanted to remove our honor and reputation.

No longer able to tolerate such a social unfairness, my soul and blood, which were already bad during my childhood, got worse. A voice cried out: "Remember that when you were a child you had something in mind, it is time to work on that and not to be coward anymore." I had been thinking of a question of honor for a long time: I got rid of the man who for so many days had been a problem to me, and later passing through Mola, Caserta, Avellino, I arrived at my sister's house in Rionero.

At night I knocked at the door.

"Who is there?" a timid voice asked.

"Open the door, my dear, it's me" I replied moved.

"Carminuccio, you are here, at this time! What did you do, run away, immediately; the news of your crime reached this place, yesterday, Don Luigi told me about that; did you kill one of your companions, don't you?"

At that moment I was afraid, I hugged and kissed my beloved sister, I advised her to remain honest and afterwards I went out on the street. Don Peppino, the buster, who had bargained over my sister's honor, did nothing at the club, where every night we gambled with impunity. Being in a dark corner near his house door, I calmly waited for the victim; that libertine was punished with the use of a dagger.

After taking revenge I worked in the countryside where I had three other colleagues, they were wanted by justice, as well.

Hidden in the thickest woods, we attacked everyone passing before our eyes, robbing the travelers, stealing their money and horses. I was captured by Del Carretto's men, I was sentenced to a severe punishment and sent to penal servitude.

CHAPTER THREE – A POLITICAL BANDIT

Garibaldi's victories made the so-called Basilicata liberals raise up; the secret committees that were owned by Corleto had trained the masses to rise up against the bourbon bad government, so in all countries everyone was preparing their weapons, was creating cartridges to be ready to fight in the designated time.

I thought the time of my moral rehabilitation had arrived. After being sentenced to a severe punishment for killing a coward, who had tried to dishonor my only sister, I kept on killing the martinets thanks to my strength and my cunning, earning my freedom with more blood, earning my life with robberies and aggressions. Under a new government, proclaimed liberal, in the bustle of a general revolution, in moments of enthusiasm and joy, I hoped of living a new life, regaining my lost freedom, for the honor of my family, so taking advantage of the popular uprisings I took part in the revolutionary revolt, mingling with Rionero rebels.

It is not my job to describe the history of the Basilicata insurrection, other people who are learned and scholars have written volumes on the subject, which I did not read and will not read, but I can say, without any doubt, that in those days I did not commit more dishonest acts, I did my duty always and everywhere, showing my bravery and boldness also in the greatest dangers. I was eager of my rehabilitation especially in order to show it to my countrymen, and to demonstrate that I was ready to give my blood for the liberal idea, so I tried everything to distinguish me from the others and to have close friends who could testify for me at the right time.

But it had been written that I could not have peace; my mother had said that I would have become a snake, and I had to poison my country and my beautiful region as a poisonous reptile does, and to make me famous for my predatory acts.

The spies who had served S. M. Francesco II, even if changed their master did not change their job; Don Vincenzo C.'s relatives were afraid that my presence in Rionero could bring harm to the tranquility of their families; the brothers of the lord I killed because he was trying to seduce my sister, also joined the others and they all together caused my collapse.

I had been living quietly in the country for two months, and I was sure to have been forgiven for my previous crimes when, in November 1860, I was secretly warned that there was a warrant of arrest for me, by the royal judicial authority.

I understood the danger that threatened me and without wasting time I saved myself, working in the countryside. I had just hatred and desire for blood in me, I hoped in a rehabilitation that perhaps would have failed later because of my nature; it was cut off, instead, not for my will, but for my enemies' infamy, therefore a desire for revenge and a need to live grew inside me.

I joined the others, who were in the same situation as mine, and after choosing the Monticchio forest as my place, began to assault the travelers with my rifle.

The absolute lack of soldiers, the poor service of the guards made me audacious and brave quickly, giving us the opportunity of having rich confiscations, onerous rewards, abundant earnings. Protected by the wooded land, aided by the local shepherds and woodcutters, by destitute people who were really miserable, my little band grew in number by recruiting fugitives from the national prisons, who were the defaulters of the justice, those who had failed to report for military service, the Royal Army deserters. But with the increase of their number, the needs to survive and to protect themselves increased, as well, and later it was also necessary to collect the offense tools. And then by running in the countryside we began to steal horses and weapons; so that very quickly I was in charge of twenty well-armed and better equipped bandits, who had already understood how to behave in a clash against the Atella soldiers.

It was necessary to take advantage of everything that could be beneficial to our survival, to look for the help of the shepherds and of the poor, to exploit our men's ignorance, so that they could consider us as victims of injustice, not as normal wrongdoers; we needed to defend an idea, a value and look for the help of those who were not satisfied with their condition and had a lot of bitterness in their hearts and the will to rebel in their minds.

The desire to rebel was a powerful weapon to me and it made me become strong and dreaded.

Even if I had not received a literary education, I was very smart and I soon understood the huge advantages that I could have by becoming an auctioneer of a reactionary struggle. With the help of skilled people, I gathered all those who had received harm because of the revolution, from the most fanatical Bourbon, to the mellifluous liberals, from the employees, who had lost their salary, to the priests and monks, furious for the law against the clergy's possessions.

Secretly aided by all of them, the poor goats' shepherd was gradually gaining power and prestige, so that the name of Crocco was greeted with enthusiasm in all the countrysides set in Melfi, as for Masaniello in Naples.

And after so many years in prison, I still feel excited when I think about the first days of 1861, when from the Lagopesole forest, to Ginestra, Barile, Ripacandida, everywhere in Melfi I was acclaimed as a novel liberator and welcomed with triumphant honors.

My men's cry of honor was a cheer for Francesco II (who I hated a lot), the emblem of a white flag with blue ribbons; we were secretly provided with weapons; some of our horses had been stolen, the others were gifts. The reactionary Committees with secret enrollments provided us with men, so, I had under my control a small army very quickly, which I regularly commanded, as I was the General officially elected and recognized by all the employees. I promised everything to each of them, including honor and fame; I promised the farmers that they would have earned their masters' lands, I told the shepherds that they would have obtained the assigned herds; I promised those lords who had become poor that they would have regained their past wealth and their dismantled castles, I promised all of them a lot of gold and honorary positions.

And so while I was exploiting a lot of poor, ignorant and ambitious people, the respectable clergy and Bourbons were exploiting me to get a head start in the reaction.

The lack of regular troops in the countries that I passed, encouraged the more hesitant people to take part into the reaction; in every corner of Basilicata people talked about an imminent fight done by Franceschiello's soldiers, supported by Austria, Spain, and tacitly aided by France, actually people rumored that a large army, after subduing Puglia, was heading for Basilicata victoriously and triumphantly.

Gradually I almost involuntarily became the head of the reactionary riots and took part in them, sure to gain money and fame from there. Skillfully prepared, the reactionary uprising started on the 7th of April at Ginestra. When those participating, including farmers, herders, citizens of all ages and conditions heard the cry "Long live to Francesco II," rushed to arm themselves with rifles, an ax, farmhouse and compact tools.

We headed for Ripacandida. The news that the moving guards from Avigliano and Rionero were against us, brought some dismay in my people; it was right at the beginning of the expedition, not to expose myself to an easy defeat, fighting against the soldiers in the open countryside. Even a partial defeat would have greatly affected the people's spirit, by removing the popular enthusiasm, that, little by little I had been able to make rise everywhere thanks to my hard work. I preferred a cunning war rather than an open and cruel fight, so, after leaving the road, I went in the woods where the ambush and victory would have been easy.

Ginestra was my empire, the safe place, the center of my strength, and from there I moved to Ripacandida. I showed my violence and cruelty, I became the master of the soldiers' barracks and I took their weapons. The wild crowd that I commanded was unable to slow down and I did not do anything to mitigate it.

My desire to destroy and loot gave me more strength, and my deeds attracted other people eager to make a fortune thanks to the blood.

So I left each one of them free of doing everything they wanted, provided that they respected our companions' families.

In the conflict against the local soldiers, their leader fell dead and his corpse, dragged through the streets, was brought before his family's house while the crowd ransacked it. The revelry and robbery lasted for more than two hours and only in the evening I decided to mitigate that drunk crowd.

My first job was to decree the ruling authority's decay, and after gathering the gang leaders all together, I appointed a temporary junta that had to sit at the city hall and emanate from there decrees and proclamations. I wanted Tedeum to be sung in all the churches in honor of the victory, and the new government's coat of arms to be eliminated, giving importance to the Bourbon's ones, that had already been abandoned.

The walk from Ripacandida to Barile was very short; numerous requests called me there to relieve the populace from the rich and the domineerings' filths, so I began that work very soon, and after taking possession of the country, I organized that government as I had done for Ripacandida.

The victories of those early days had rightly alarmed the gentlemen, but had attracted thousands of farmers, as well, so they ran to me from everywhere to be commanded by me. I understood that I should, without wasting time, take possession of the most important centers, so I sent some men I trusted to Venosa so that they could set the stage.

And on the 10th, in the morning, with my little army of predators, I moved to conquer the venerable Venosa.

I knew that the town (8000 inhabitants) was prepared to protect itself and San Gervasio Palace soldiers had arrived to help the civil guard, but I knew that my coming to the country was expected by many people, most of them being gentlemen, and the others being populace.

At halfway, I was informed that the civic militia, alarmed because of my soldiers, had decided to close the doors, to barricade the streets, to go and occupy the castle.

Arrived near the city, I divided my army in different groups and I assigned a sector of attack to each of them; while I was engaged in this operation, I saw some white weathercocks waving from the top of the churches, which was a familiar signal, so I definitely ordered the attack.

But it was a bloodless attack, as after climbing over the walls the doors were opened without the need of a shot, and I entered with my soldiers occupying the main square, from where I moved to attack the castle.

Thanks to my soldiers' cries of joy and of fury, along with the popular acclaim, the defense understood that their efforts were vain; a few rifle shots fired at the walls made the surrender be obtained, with the promise that everyone would have gone on living.

Venosa was mine and very quickly I received the congratulations of everyone, as well as every kind of supplications.

I took care of opening the jails, appointing a ruling Council and publishing the names of those whose properties and lives had to be respected, the violator would have been punished.

From the 10th to the 14th I stayed with my relatives in Venosa stripping, looting, imposing rewards, destroying men and houses, killing all those who were enemies of the reaction.

After Venosa we decided to occupy Melfi, where our friends had made all the possible efforts so that I would have been welcomed with the honors of my degree.

On April 14th 1861 I left Venosa and I headed for Lavello acclaimed by those people with the cry "Long live to Francesco II."

Collected in the little country what we were able to find, because of the limited resources, and appointed the usual Commission ruling the Town Hall, I headed for Melfi where the royal power had been declared decayed by the popular plebiscite.

In spite of many disappointments I found during my brave life, I remember with great pleasure the main one, the most beautiful one, which accompanied my entry into the city of Melfi, capital of the district. Someone reading these memories could consider my writing exaggerated, but I swear not on my honor, but on my mother's sacred memory, that I am not exaggerating, that I do not lie, and the official documents can prove it.

At the feet of the long hill that led to the front door, leaving the roadway, I was welcomed with the sound of music, by a committee composed of the wealthiest people in the city, while the bells were tolling, and from the balconies, crowded with people and wallpapers with colorful tapestries, the women were throwing flowers and kisses.

Once at the main square, Mr.... from his sumptuous palace after a speech underlying the virtues and glories of the Bourbon government, invited the people to acclaim Crocco, the proud general of the good King Francesco II.

An "Hurrah to Crocco" replied to that invitation, while on the streets some firecrackers were shot as a sign of happiness.

In the church, richly adorned for me, the Madonna del Carmine had been exposed, so that I paid a devout homage to the Virgin Mary who had protected me and turned me into a winner, unharmed man after so many bitter struggles. In the evening of my entry, there were lights, parties, dances and revelry in the whole town.

Since in Melfi, as I said before, the restoration had been done before my arrival, I found that all the appropriate measures have been enacted, actually those gentlemen had already destroyed all archives (my mortal enemies) and opened the prisons, as I usually did.

In addition, showing the utmost respect to me, they wanted that I approved their work, which I did by approving all the regulations given and taken.

The enemies of the restoration were exiled, their properties were confiscated, their houses were looted; in order to protect the public order a special service was created using the most faithful men of my gang. They had to constrain my robbers and prevent bloody scenes, the transgressors would have been punished with death. And because an example was essential, I remember I publicly shot a man from Atella, who had ransacked the house of a reactionary person.

Using the weapons seized in Venosa and in Melfi as well as the horses gathered on the way, I organized all that crowd following me and divided it into centurions, under the command of a captain, and into regiments under the command of colonels.

Two centurions rode horses under the command of a major.

But unfortunately I could not enjoy the idleness of Melfi for more days, as I was informed that from Bari, from Potenza and Foggia a lot of regular troops were marching against me. I realized very soon that if it had been easy to me to fight against the civic militia and to attack defenseless cities prepared to surrender with my army of bandits, it would have been impossible to fight outdoors against regular troops, equipped with artillery and cavalry. Neither I could gather all those people who had followed me, so after a right selection among the volunteers, I gave freedom to the less helpful and in the night of the 18th of April, with tears in my eyes and bile in my heart, I left Melfi heading for Avellino.

While the troops of King Vittorio Emanuele arrived in Melfi on the 19th (a battalion of the 30th and one of the 5th infantry), I attacked a little village named Carbonara, forcing people to give me food for my people and gold for the pay.

In Calitri after a fierce struggle against the villagers, I had a wonderful victory and with a large reward to the municipality and to the owners, I filled our cases, preparing a good store of money for my days off.

The arrival of the first regular troops had relieved the depressed spirits of the civic guards, so the soldiers already on the way organized themselves in a better way under the command of brave citizens, and helped the other soldiers with the repression. At the same time the rigor of the military commanders, who had perceived severe penalties that were against all those who helped in any way the reaction or the drifter reactionaries, had a great influence not only on the reduction my band, but also on the decrease of the support of the confidants and the spies.

After stifling the reactionary uprisings everywhere, after the various countries had come back into the orbit of the law, the liberals' audacity grew in the various centers and in the public circles where people talked about us as a terror of the population, treated us as shepherds, as worthless individuals, who ran away at the sight of a rifle.

I had occupied the village of Sant'Andrea, where I had decided to stop for a few days to let the band rest, when I heard from a confidant that in the village of Conza the commander of the National Guard had, the evening before, uttered aloud words of contempt toward me, adding that with his soldiers he felt able to make me run away with my band. In order to punish such a great pride my bosses advised me to destroy Conza; I did not agree, and after calling a fellow soldier, I ordered him to mount a horse and give the following letter to the mayor of Conza:

"Gentlemen of Conza.

"I occupy as you well know, Sant'Andrea with my band. I encourage you, if you don't want me to come there, to send me the tricolor flag of the municipality, the pictures of King Vittorio Emanuele and Garibaldi being in the board room, as well as the land case.

"Everything must be sent to me by the Commander of the National Guard himself.

"I give you eight hours. Carmine Crocco, General of Francesco II."

Six hours later the commander was depressed at my feet begging for pity for his old mother who would have died of grief, and thinking of my mother, I decided to save his life.

At the beginning of May, finding it difficult to find food for the strength of my band, and willing to run away from the national troops and guards who were following me, I divided my band into several parts setting the Lagopesole woods as the place to gather all together.

The call to the old Neapolitan classes to be mixed with the other troops of the Army, gave me the opportunity to have a great element in my crowd.

At the beginning of June the reservists had to go to the storage to wear the military uniform, but most of them preferred to devote themselves to the countryside instead of following the army, and so I had the chance of hiring more experienced men, and those accustomed to the labors of the fields and to discipline.

The riots were quickly stifled and did not leave deep traces in the various countries. Those who had to mitigate the reaction were able to win thanks to their strength and clemency: the few victims of counter-reaction were due to the local enemies and revenges, rather than to the rigor of a law that was supposed to be martial.

Many of those who had shouted, "Long live to Francesco II," "Hurrah for Crocco," when the troops arrived, shouted "Hurrah for Vittorio", "Hurrah for Cialdini," and they were considered as liberals while we believed they were reactionaries.

Being the head of the reaction I would have deserved to die, but as I was young and I loved the life, I thought it was right to protect it with all the possible efforts of my strong body, so after leaving the politics and the politicians, I returned to my first job of common robber, forced to attack the travelers, to impose rewards to let me and my band survive.

I found out later, even if I did not know if it was true or not, that among those who had helped to look for justice, there was the knight Giulio Roland, governor of the province, and the sub-prefect Decio Lordi, who had provided me with the weapons and the horses to fight in favor of the revolution.

Therefore, it was not my fault if I had easily changed my mind; the example I followed came from above, from those who had to be an example.

I wrote several times to the Knight Roland urging him to meet each other as I wanted to resolve an old problem, inviting him to continue with his job, because he would have had a fast career and the gratitude of my countrymen, always happy to be poor and horned because of the Piedmont work.

I had the opportunity to resolve the issue with the sub-prefect; but the devil was always there, and that lucky individual escaped from me just when I was thinking of his torture.

But I don't want to hasten the events.

CHAPTER FOUR – THE BANDITS' GENERAL

On the 10th of August 1861 I introduce me to you, kind reader, not as a recognized leader of the reactionary riots, but as the general of a formidable band of bandits.

I have a plumed hat, a useless tunic, a pure black horse, a lot of weapons, and in addition, I have the command of more than a thousand men, who move and act when I want.

At the beginning of the day I get close to a village, named Ruvo del Monte, located on the slope of a hill, shaded by leafy chestnut trees, by fertile vineyards. Here and there I run into little but nice and big villas. Far from here there is a huge tower, which overlooks the ruined feudal castle, and reveals the antiquity of the village.

I am in charge of 1,200 men and 175 horses; the bells of the parish are tolling, which is a sure indication that the inhabitants are preparing for the defense of their lives, of their wealth and their honor. I stop at a half-mile away from the first houses and write to the Mayor and to the Board the following letter:

"Dear Mr. Mayor and Gentlemen of Ruvo del Monte. "I'm here in your presence, not to hurt you, but rather to pray you so that your lordships have the goodness to give me the forage for 1,200 men and 175 horses, I will pay in gold for it.

"After that I will continue my journey; I hope that you, respectable men, satisfy my prayers, not obliging me to be violent. I give you one hour to answer.

I am Carmine Donatello Crocco" After half an hour I get the following response:

"Dear Carminuccio. "We simply cannot accept the request made to us; it not only affects our reputation according what the Royal Government thinks but touches our heart and our self-respect, as well. And since we are well supplied with cartridges and we want to test our courage and our dust, we expect that you come forward with your shepherds and we will kill them.

"The best advice that we can give you is that you go away, and soon, as there will be soon some soldiers from Rionero, from San Fele and Calitri. They will follow you and it will be over for you and yours."

"Mayor Biasucci»

After reading this letter to my teammates, I said to them: "Young men, we must punish not only this rejection, but also the insult to call us shepherds by killing them, those who are brave can follow me." I arranged four centurions on the front line, which furiously headed for the country, and were welcomed by a fire of musketry well fed but not very strong, while another 200 men were ordered to attack the side area. The knights were to control the road to Rionero and to move forward in time to inform me about the troops' arrival; another centurion was directed to the road of Calitri with the same instructions. The remaining men under the command of Ninco Nanco were left behind for the revival. The attack was simultaneous and terrible. In eternal honor of those brave citizens who fell, I can assure you that they fought in every inch of their village. After losing their first position, they were stationed in the square; after being forced to leave that area, as well, they occupied the area near the church and after firing all the cartridges, they fought against my soldiers. Overwhelmed by the number, they tried to reach the tower, but as the street was closed, they prepared to die, but the women, crying, threw themselves among the fighters begging for mercy and grace for their fathers, their husbands and their children. A white flag waved on the tower, so the fight ended, but the streets were crowded with corpses, and my men ransacked everything.

The municipal authority was sitting, so when I walked in the palace of the town, I found the councilors in their place.

I ordered that the role of the National Guard, the guns and the soldiers' ammunitions, the common fund and that of the land, were given to me. I was replied that I had to put an end to the bloodsheds and the fire, and I would have been satisfied. It was done that way.

Recalling that famous day I still wonder where those poor citizens had learned the art of the war, as to explain their strength and their ability to fight, being about 300, for several hours against 1000 young men, eager for pleasure and the prey.

Those brave men had never participated in small or large fights, actually the ferocity of the Bourbon government forbade them to take the gun, and in order to take arms they had to pay 5 ecus. Why were the Bourbons unable to use so a spontaneous value and heroism, in their strong region, so that the powerful Bourbon army was forced to escape from some young men? Why were they called heroes and the others vile? The truth of those easy victories, the cause of the escapes, the easy deviation, and so on!

You should have seen a military Bourbon district; and I saw it and understood everything. I saw how many infamies were committed, and the whip, the cane and the executions, and the terrible punishments, so that we as soldiers thought: "This is your and your men's kingdom, protect it with the help of your soldiers, and I will die for your glory and to keep the crown on your head."

But someone will say, and they will be right, that you knew the Bourbons' infamies, but after their fall, you fell into the mud and put yourself and your mates at the mercy of a cause, which had aroused in you so much horror.

I do not want people to talk about me, but I had already killed some people, I was searched, I struggled to live, I was the snake remembered by my poor mother, who died insane in the mental hospital of Aversa.

Let's go back to Ruvo. In the evening I left the village and headed for the hills of Frunti just a mile from the first buildings. At night from all the neighboring countries some stagecoaches reached me, and I understood the countries' discouragement or the dispatches' departure to unite the forces against me, so I assumed that the next day I would not have been disturbed. So the following day I organized a new company of recruits with magnificent rifles from Ruvo; I raised the number of the cavalry to 190 with 15 horses stolen from the Ruvo; around noon the leader of the band Agostino Sacchitello arrived with 162 men and 60 horses, all armed with splendid rifles and numerous ammunitions, so that all together we reached the strength of 1541 men and 256 horses, the best ones of Puglia.

On the 11th I was told that the government authority was doing something. The command of the force was in Rionero, where there were numerous platoons of various detachments. If I remember correctly, there was a battalion of riflemen, one of the 62nd infantry, three battalions of mobile guards, two companies of the 32nd infantry and the National Guard.

The command had decided to vigorously attack me using the encirclement. They knew that I was wounded, but did not think that the wounded tiger frightens the hunter.

Sure not to be molested, in the afternoon I headed for Ruvo where I had my wound treated, and in the evening with the fanfare in my head I headed for the river Ofanto, in the direction of Calitri. Everyone thought that I was moving to occupy Calitri, actually late at night, I unexpectedly changed direction and after three hours of backwards, I stopped in a position that seemed to me very strong.

This position was made of a woody mass, protected in front of it and laterally to the right, by the steep banks of a river called

Vomina, while at the back and to the left there was an extended plain, which allowed the cavalry to maneuver.

In this position, I decided to wait for the troops, ready to die rather than abandon it.

At dawn the next day the troops arrived at Ruvo, and because of the news of my departure and the direction taken, decided to follow me, sure to surprise me in the woods of Castiglione or in those of Monticchio.

My spies, after accompanying the troops up to the Ofanto, informed me that they had rested in Scona, eight miles away from me.

To better strengthen me in the position taken, I thought about building a stilt house, about 400 meters from the front line, shaped like a half moon. Briefly explained the purpose of the defense to my men, I ordered to build it and in a while two hundred axes began to cut bushes, so that in a few hours I had a strong shelter been built for the shooters, who were still covered in front of the bare grasslands where the road that leads from Melfi to Naples passed.

At about two o'clock p.m., the sub-prefect Decio Lordi from Muro Lucano, received the exchange, left Melfi to take the sub-prefecture of Eboli. Escorted by a moving guard company and a dozen of martinets, he was riding along the road, when I was informed of him, and I ordered my nights to attack him.

Surprised by a brilliant tension, the soldiers of the guard had to give up without fighting, while the lucky Decio barely escaped with two martinets thanks to the speed of his horse. In that conflict three soldiers were killed and six were wounded.

A young lieutenant from San Fele was in charge of the group and thanks to him, the survived National Guard, in spite of my soldiers' desire for blood, was able to come back to his country, alive. That lieutenant's father had once benefited from my father, so I saved his life and that of his men.

Before saying goodbye, I begged the officer to do homage to the commander from Piedmont who was following me, and to warn him that I would have waited for him at the Toppacivita brush, where I would have stayed for some days.

Back in the village, the official told the happened adventure, because soon after I received a letter, written in: Rionero in Vulture, August 13th, 1861:

"Mr. Carmine Donatelli Crocco.

"Thanks for the freedom given to my employees killed by your weapons. Once more, for the country's sake, for many families' sake and for your sake, I invite you to abandon your arms and I assure you that you will not be executed and your case will be referred to the sovereign authorities. Tomorrow we will not come there to give you time to reflect. If, in spite of this letter, you persist in being rebellious to the law, I will be forced, against my will, to follow you and catch you, dead or alive.

"P. C. "

"Gentlemen, sincere regards.

"I cannot absolutely adhere to your request because S. M. Vittorio Emanuele has rejected the request of the lawyer Mr. Francesco Guarini and will reject the others, in spite of being supported by your lordship. And since I don't want to be a plaything for those who will be present at my execution, so I'm ready to sell my life at great cost.

"Remember that in this place, in 1808, an entire regiment of King Gioacchino Murat was slaughtered.

"Carmine Crocco»

By keeping his word, the Commander from Piedmont was idle for 24 hours, hoping that I changed my advice; this time was very precious to me because I had the opportunity to strengthen myself in my small fortified camp. I saw with pleasure how ardently my shepherds were working; they had understood how useful that sort of hedge, made of poles, bundles, earth and stones, could be, and by measuring the height, the strength, were making predictions about the imminent battle. Coppa, the most ferocious man of all, had sworn to get drunk with blood, as he had done in Caiazzo, the others, less ferocious compared to him, made their brutal promises, and everyone was driven by an ardent desire to fight.

I was sure to win and this let me feel extremely calm, even the less brave were not afraid of being attacked, so in everyone there was more the certainty of the next triumph rather than an alive hope.

You don't have to believe, however, that my men were all shepherds. I had a small and perfect army with supervisors, a captain, a lieutenant, a doctor, sergeants, corporals, all belonging to the dissolved Bourbon army. I had six hundred soldiers of all units, hunters, cavalry, artillery, vaulters, sappers, miners, and guard grenadiers and so on that. What does it matter if they were shepherds, farmers, peasants? The current armies are all composed of children of the wretched populace. If I had to choose between two regiments, one of students, the other of shepherds or farmers, I would always choose the second, because they are accustomed to the cold, the hunger, the hard work, and to walk. I'm not saying that students are vile; no, I will never say such an infamous slander, but I prefer the rough man, the peasant, who is easier to train, more prepared to obey, less demanding about food, and unable to criticize the orders received.

Warned by the spies of the advance of the troops, I made my knights leave the field, I divided them into five platoons who headed for five different directions, with the specific mission to explore far away and report back.

We were six miles far from the soldiers, therefore, as soon as the troop left Porta of Naples, from our high position, we were able to observe it thanks to our good telescopes and follow its movements.

At the beginning of the day the weapons and the officers' uniforms were shimmering in the sun; my soldiers were on mules or on horses; they had a shoulder blue scarf, a gun at their side and someone had a rifle on their shoulders.

While the soldiers were advancing silently, I thought of that commander from Piedmont and of his officers, who had a poor concept of us from the South, they all believed we were vile and that way they treated those people who gave them hospitality.

"You'll see, you'll see what my shepherds will be able to do," I murmured to myself. "Here among ourselves you will not find the luxury of lined rifles, but old guns, not sharp and barbed sabers, but cutting axes, flintlock pistols, long daggers, Catalans knives. Without the luxury of smart uniforms, actually ragged and naked, barefoot or with canvas shoes, Calabria style hats, cartridge belts, we only look shepherds but we are ready to fight on a par."

And with those thoughts I got ready to fight. I stationed 800 men, the best armed and the most resolute, behind the stilt; about 300 meters away, into the woods, I placed 200 men armed with shotguns, who had to protect the retreat in case of defeat, while I placed another 200 men on the side, indoors, to attack at the decisive moment. Each group of 200 men was commanded by a chief, called captain, who was in charge of lieutenants and sergeants. For every 10 individuals there was a corporal. The unarmed men, because of lack of rifles, were responsible for transporting the wounded from the stilts to the big woods.

These things done, I talked to the old captain Antonio Bosco, to the Lieutenant Francesco N., to the Lieutenant Luigi Siciliano and to the old non-commissioned officers of the Bourbon army, and we unanimously agreed that our positions were formidable and that only the artillery could have attacked us.

I left the command to the captain Bosco, who, after swearing an oath, I appointed colonel, and after deciding to be in charge of the knights, I moved against the troops with the intention of gradually attracting them near the place where my soldiers were stationed, behind the fence. In case of defeat the retreat was to head for Monticchio towards the church of St. Michele.

Addressing to my old colleagues, already accustomed to the sound of the lead, I ordered them to mount on horses and get ready for the endeavour. They were the fierce Ninco Nanco, the bloodthirsty Giovanni Coppa, Agostino Sacchetiello, his brother Vito, Giuseppe Schiavone, Michele Di Biase, Tortora Donato Teschetta, Gambini, Palmieri, Cavalcante, Serravalle, Teodori, D'Amato, Caruso, Sorotonde and others.

At the head of these famous bandits there was the snake, my mother's prophecy was right. Divided into five squads, we headed for the Atella bridge where we stopped on a hill rising above the torrent. From the top position, I could see the advance of the troops; the church of St. Lucia was already occupied by the infantry and other troops had crossed the churchyard.

As usual, the first to appear was the battalion of riflemen, which with admirable courage crossed the torrent and moving against us began to open a brisk fire and after the cry of "Savoia", using a fixed bayonet, it started the attack.

We certainly did not remain without doing anything. Twelve revolver rifles, arrived in the evening from Naples along with sixty English revolvers had to be tested, and they were the first to be used against the sharpshooters.

I saw with my own eyes a corporal falling died, another soldier falling to the ground mortally wounded, the major's horse hit in the chest falling and rising any more; but the sharpshooters as real possessed men were always advancing, so it was necessary to leave our position and retreat to a beautiful plain.

Taking advantage of a momentary division being in the battalion who had attacked us, when the soldiers had arrived at the top of the hill we at first occupied and then abandoned, I ordered the knights to move back into the fight and to return to the fray.

Our rapid movement surprised the sharpshooters who tiredly advanced in dribs and drabs, and produced a great disorder, and they would have suffered a lot if a battalion of the 62nd infantry had not dampened our ardor, forcing us to run away. After a mile of gallop, we conquered the farm Mezzanotte.

The troops had given the signal alt and the battalion of the 62nd infantry, who had followed us, was ordered to retire and went to join the other troops in the plane named Cartolico.

I took advantage of the momentary truce to look at my men, the sharpshooters had killed one of our companions and had wounded six men; among our horses, sixteen were wounded some because of a dagger and the others because of rifles; I sent the wounded to my little entrenched camp, and afterwards we recharged our batteries, tightened the straps to the horses, and, lying as a cord, we decided to observe.

A battalion of the National Guard moved before us and arrived within range opened the fire; we answered soon and at the first shots, as I learned afterwards, the son of my uncle, Michele Crocco, collector of the land, died. The fight was bold by both sides, it was a pleasure to see so numerous shots shaking up the dry land, but, all in a sudden, two groups slithering on the ground without being seen arrived at our right side and attacked our bayonet.

That unexpected clash confused my knights, who at full speed retreated followed by the troop.

But as the soldiers were on foot and we were on horses it was easy to go far from them, and afterwards, using different shepherds' huts, we waited in ambush.

The troop advancing rapidly reached us, and feeling that we were behind the huts, began to shoot, and after the cry of "Savoia" there was the assault.

But the cunning and the art of deception prevailed on value. A half of us pretended to retreat and was chased; the other half turning from left to right, with rapid movements reached the side, and after breaking the central part, forced those who were at the end to retreat, while the beginning part was fighting against my soldiers, suddenly returned to the assault.

Come back after the unexpected trap, the group was able to return to their initial state when we were already gone. In this battle, my horse was wounded by the shot of a bayonet, named Vito, from Avigliano, the province of Potenza, who after having fought against us as a true lion, feeling surrounded, pretended to abandon his rifle, and while my companion approached him to get the weapon, he with a fast movement, hit him in his side with his bayonet; at this sight, I, who was close, shot at point-blank range.

Struck in the chest he turned against me and shot me with his bayonet, but he hit my horse. Shortly after that fierce man died.

My aim was to gradually attract the troops near my soldiers who were stationed close to the stilt, as the retreat and the escapes had an usual direction. The battalion of the National Guard who had always followed us with admirable vigor, went near my stationed companions and was greeted with a terrible shot. Very quickly, the road was covered with dead and wounded men; the soldiers, as being not able to assault, and being impossible to overcome the torrent's steep banks, beyond which there were my soldiers, it was inevitable to respond with fire to our fire. And in fact the action lasted for some time, then the armed citizens retreated heading for the troops at the back that were advancing toward our right side.

My tired soldiers and I, along with 19 prisoners, entered the small fortress where I found everything in perfect order. My friends envied us and complained that they were waiting too long, and that they were not accustomed to that.

I reassured everyone, telling them that before long they would have had the opportunity to fight. "Do not doubt, I told them, because soon you will be luckier than us. Look at the enemy commander who quietly follows us, as a hermit who recites the rosary. Who knows what that old man from Crimea is thinking about. Do you know what makes me tremble? It's his cold blood, it's his calm behavior. How I would like to kill him, not so much for the pleasure of seeing his blood, but to show him and let him know how in the provinces of our unfortunate country, there are men who are worth as the other men of the earth are; to teach these bad people from Piedmont, who wittily call us "stubborn, cowards, peasants, rude, ignorant and bigots," that we are brave and have a heart, as well. These things said, I wanted to give an account of the situation and added: "We had two deaths, a prisoner, twenty-seven wounded and twenty-one horses unable to fight anymore. In turn, we seized twenty soldiers, seventy-five rifles and several ammunitions, they will count the dead men. What can we do with the prisoners? If we are attacked, we will be forced to flee, who is alive has the duty, before running away, to kill as many soldiers as they can, at least the dead will not speak; on the contrary if we will not be bothered, I will ask for an exchange of prisoners.

"You, Giovanni, Giuseppe and Agostino Schiavone, mount on horse very quickly, go to Beppe, Ninco Nanco, gather the staff all together, leave there only twenty people under the command of Andreotto with the duty to keep the position from that side. Carry with you the rest of the staff occupying the hill Caprareccia di Mezzanotte.

"Arrived there you have to let a group of twenty people go outside with the duty to control the hills of Cartoffo, the road and the valley of the farm. If the Commander from Piedmont sent you one of his battalions, your task would not be that of working hard, in fact you would have to attract him near the place where our soldiers are stationed, pretending to retreat. The riders will head for the castle trying to keep busy the battalion of riflemen. I'll take care of the rest."

While I was saying to my soldiers these words, the troop evidently tired, was resting. The officers gathered all together, with the topographic maps in their hands, heard the signal of "attention!", and formed a column, the troop advanced towards us.

"There they are!, I exclaimed, they are advancing against our position with the intention of shooting each of us, brothers, be brave, let them see that we, as shepherds, know how to meet them and that we are ready to cut their throats, as we are able to butcher the kids. Be brave, then, I am with you; if we were to move out of here, I'll always be the last to get out. "

The attack was initiated by a battalion of the Mobile Guard reinforced by a battalion of the National Guard. After a strong fire, the Mobile Guard started the assault, greeted by a deadly fire, made by my men stationed on the stilt. Baffled by an unexpected resistance, that battalion halted, and, shaken by the numerous losses, turned back.

But in order to reinforce the soldiers the good battalion of the 62nd infantry arrived; this battalion composed mostly of Piedmont men, old soldiers accustomed to war, did not act like our mobilized soldiers, advanced with perfect order fighting with an indifference that scared me. Fearless, attacked the front part and arrived halfway up, the soldiers stationed on the ground, starting a slow but precise shooting against us, with the intention of getting us tired with the fire, forcing us to finish our ammunitions and afterwards they attacked us with their bayonets.

I called a reinforcement of 200 men in reserve, which I took on the fire line, ordering them to save their ammunitions. The battalion of the Mobile Guard, following the strong example of the 62nd infantry was reorganized, as well, and with a rapid change began to attack on my left wing, while at almost the same time, the 62nd infantry at the cry "Savoia" attacked the stilt . I don not remember what happened next; a terrible noise, screams, curses mixed with the moans of the wounded, clouds of smoke raised high and covered a space of hundreds of meters, which prevented us from seeing what was going on.

A captain and twelve soldiers after bravely entering the stilt, were killed by our soldiers while everywhere around there the fight was going on. Finally, the commander's trumpet sounded and we retreated, and it meant our survival, as a minute later my soldiers would have certainly escaped from that ferocious fight, indeed many of them had already retreated and returned only when they were informed of our victory thanks to our cries of joy.

It was a quarter to 12 and we had been standing the attack of the tripled troop for 8 hours, under the rays of the sun. If the very strong difference between our large number of soldiers and the little number of petty battalions that had attacked us had not made us so strong and brave, perhaps on that day my band would have been exterminated. And in spite of such a large difference of strength, we would have been ruined, as well, if the Commander of Piedmont, had not made the mistake of not making the riflemen take part into the assault, leaving them idle in reserve to control my knights.

A lack of chivalry in the troop contributed to our salvation; a platoon of brave knights would have had a great influence with his accurate information by ensuring that it would not have been useless to fight against a strong and well defended position.

It was right to let the officers and the troops realize that that fight had not frightened us morally and materially, so I ordered the commander of my knights to cross the stream very quickly and move forward, heading for the farm Occhio di Lupo.

The Commander of Piedmont, despite the sweltering heat, the exhaustion of his soldiers and the late hour, decided to do the last attack, and in order to do it he took the sharpshooters off from the reserve, which was replaced with 500 men of the National Guard. The fierce Giuseppe Nicola Summa, said Ninco-Nanco, whose name alone put fear into the population, realized that thanks to his cunning behavior, knowing very well that those soldiers were armed with hunting rifles without bayonets, and that the mass was composed of fathers in general, and of a lot of angry bourbons, become liberals in spite of their will, Ninco Nanco decided to attack them with his men on horses. After saying that, he did that, crossed a covered path, approached unnoticed and afterwards furiously fought on his horseback.

Surprised by that audacity, the soldiers dispersed and the regular troop had to rush to their aid, while Ninco Nanco with his men went in a safe place, by turning back.

This unexpected attack convinced the commander of Piedmont to leave us in peace for that day at least, and in fact the troop came back to the country.

With my binoculars I was able to observe the troops retreating and I also saw my soldiers, now captives, who bound and escorted by the sharpshooters were in the central part.

Without wasting any time, I wrote this letter: Signorelli Manor Farm, August 14th, 1861

"Mr. Major,

"Send here a captain of the active troop and the lawyer D. Emanuele Brienza, with whom I have to talk about the fate of your men now in my power. Yours faithfully,

Carmine Donatelli Crocco»

A couple of hours later, a sergeant arrived to understand what I wanted with my letter.

I replied that I had fifty soldiers, including a captain with me, and that twelve of my companions had fallen into the troops' power; if the commander wanted to shoot my men, in turn, I would have his soldiers slaughtered, beginning with the captain, and I was willing to let them all free as long as my soldiers were left free, as well.

The news that the captain was alive has, as a consequence, the immediate return of my men, to which I replied by releasing all the soldiers in my power. The day of August 14th 1861 was fatal for us, but it was fatal also for the troop and especially for the National Guard. In the various countries of the Melfi district, many families grieved, and in the far Piedmont other families cried for the loss of a beloved person, murdered by our soldiers; and perhaps there is still some old women who say to their grandchildren, "your grandfather and your uncle was killed by robbers, and performed his duty in a honorable way; but fair God killed all the vile murderers and those who did not die being shot, died in prison."

God did not want me to die, and after 30 years, recalling all that blood, I feel in me the deepest of the sorrows which torment this miserable existence.

The bandits in the evening of August 14th 1861 being tired, rested in the position of Toppacivita which was still theirs. Reader, while my band exhausted by such a fatigue rests in the place of their victory, I want to talk to you about one of our bivouacs.

The robbers, when are not threatened by a close troop, normally sleep in the shade of leafy oaks, lying on the ground in a jumble; they have a stone or a clump as pillow, the coat or the cloak as blankets; the guns are near the plants with the cartridges attached to the stock. On the front line, at the sides, on the back, all around, advanced lookouts are carefully watching, while the secret spies are near the troops. The leaders are resting in a secluded place under huts built with branches of trees with ground and straw on soft beddings, sometimes accompanied by their lovers. In order to reinforce the lookouts stationed on the summit of a mountain, on the top of a tree, on the top of some ruined castle, there are dogs, fierce dogs that sniff out a prey at a great distance where the human sight cannot arrive. The horses, gathered in ten with halter and thread, are grazing free in the woods. The wounded, the sick of the day, are hospitalized inside the forest with plenty of straw and some rare blankets. They are treated with affection, practice compensates for science and art: the wounds are washed with water and vinegar, the drugs commonly used are: potatoes, filaments, bands, egg whites, beaten olive oil and leaves of a kind of grass called print horse.

It may seem ridiculous that the potato is an useful medicine, but it is very useful, at least the robbers consider it this way. The potatoes well beaten produce a milky ointment, which has the power to take the bad blood, the dust poisoning; it gathers the stringy flesh, makes the swelling disappear and narrows the hole. To cure the wounds provoked by sharp things or by cuts, beaten oil and pelosella leaves are used, they are abundant in arid and mountainous places.

When they have to eat, the soldiers are divided into groups, each of those is led by a group leader; on the less steep slope of the position, that has to be possibly covered so that the smoke does not betray us, the fires are lit; not far from there, the cooks are slaughtering the goats, are excoriating the pigs, are plucking the chickens and the turkeys, while the others are cutting the firewood to have abundant embers, the meat is ready to be roasted.

The food is stolen in the rich farms and villages using weapons; during the night the houses are surrounded and while some people kidnap the farmers, the others rob the stables, the roosts and the basements. The money used for the pay are provided by the reactionaries and the liberals. The first do voluntary donations while the second are forced to give them their money and if they refuse to do it, they are threatened cutting their plants, with fires, devastations and similar damages.

On August 15th 1861, the day of the Assumption, to celebrate the victory against the garrison in Rionero, I wanted on our table two hundred sheeps, a thousand chickens, two casks of wine, all stolen, for the most part, from captain Giannini from S. Fele's farm.

For the pay, the chiefs have a percentage on the rewards and the blackmails, the soldiers an amount per day, the temporary men five ecus each when they are fired.

And now that I've digressed enough with tedious and unnecessary descriptions, I return to my gestures, the predatory acts made by me in August 1861.

From the strong position of Toppacivita, after the clashes had, I had not moved, I had indeed ordered to better strengthen that palisade-shelter, to be able to overcome new attacks, while numerous diggers were breaking down the telegraph poles and cutting the wires to disrupt the communications.

The commander of the forces of Piedmont living in Rionero after measuring the strength of my band compared to that of his meager battalions, could not help but ask for reinforcements, and waiting for their arrival left us in peace.

The countrysides, rightly terrified by the carnage of my band, were deserted, the streets were deserted, the rural farms were empty. Strict military calls ordered all the citizens not to go out far from the countries after the Hail Mary of Seram, the transgressors would have been executed, so a deep squalor, a sense of sadness and desolation reigned everywhere.

This exceptional occurrence of things indirectly damaged my

band, because there was a loss of the so-called goods of the market, so I decided to leave the Toppacivita brush and find a way to live, arriving unexpectedly at small villages unprotected by the local militia and regular troops.

I attacked Rapone forcing the people to pay heavy contributions of money and food, threatened the lords from San Fele imposing blackmails and burdens, and after having forced people from Atella to pay different amounts of money, with my band reduced to about a thousand men, went into the Lagopesole bush.

Ninco Nanco

Giuseppe "Sparviero" Schiavone

CHAPTER FIVE – WITH BORJES

I lived assaulting, extorting, killing occasionally, when a shepherd from Tricarico sent me a note of the robber Serravalle where he asked me for a meeting in the Carriera farm.

It was here, in October 1861, that I met the Spanish general Börjes came by order of Francesco II to try to raise the people of the Two Sicilies. The man who was a stranger and had arrived here to recruit followers and to ask for my band's help, from the first moment aroused in my soul a strong dislike, so I quickly realized that, according to him, I had to abandon my rank of general commander of my band, to become a subordinate.

He was a poor deluded and came from his distant country to be in charge of an army. He had believed that everywhere there were insurgent people, and after a first colossal fiasco from Calabria to

Basilicata, he wanted to convince me and my soldiers that it would not have been difficult to produce a real insurrection, thanks to the number of my band, the excellent element that was in them, our good weapons and excellent horses.

The experience, teacher of life, advised me not to look for the help of the reactionaries, if I did not want to repeat another escape like that from Melfi; however, the idea of being commanded by a skilled man of war and being able to use something different from violence to conquer villages and towns, where we could have enriched ourselves with robberies and blackmails, was an encouragement not to reject the requested help.

Serravalle encouraged us to unconditionally accept Börjes' proposal, but both my soldiers and I were hesitant, rather inclined to refuse, as we were not accustomed to be subjected to military disciplines, actually we were used to live a free life and to freely steal and rob.

After long negotiations and verbal agreements about the use of force, about the organization of the command, the daily wages, I joined the Spanish general with my band, and with him I began new brigands' actions, but under the tutelage of a political movement.

Now I do not remember exactly which was the route decided by Börjes in his plan of invasion of Basilicata, he had stated his intention to attack the smallest towns, giving them a new order of government, enlisting recruits, weapons and horses and afterwards assaulting the county town, where secret committees were working to prepare weapons and armed men ready to arise when we would have attacked.

From Lagopesole, from bush to bush with long and forced marches almost always carried out at night, crossing mule roads and almost impassable paths, we reached the Basento banks, gathering many recruits in the process.

The first country to be attacked was Trivigno. On November 2nd, from the bivouac forest of the Brindisi mountain we crossed the Trivigno forest and in the evening of the 3rd at dusk we descended the country by taking an attack position, we gathered all together indoors in an old church in ruins, and exactly in a place called Calvario, which is about 200 meters far from the village.

The National Guard, a hundred soldiers, informed of our progress, boldly ran to take arms, and not aware of our strengths, stepped out of the country to fight against us.

Greeted with my soldiers' shooting, those soldiers took their position and soon responded to our fire, but their small number and uncomfortable condition compared to ours, had to retire quickly.

Back in the village, they stationed in the first houses so that they could attack us at our entrance and with a large fire made from the windows and the roofs, they forced us to retreat.

But I was not naive enough to be not prepared; I ordered a centurion to advance along the covered path, stopping at a convenient distance to open a large fire, while several platoons had to try entering the country from different directions to attack the defenders from their backs.

The really fierce fight lasted for three hours, then the brave defenders being in bad conditions because of the deficiency of ammunitions, abandoned all thoughts of defense and left the country at our mercy. The unfortunate citizens, my companions eager for blood and prey knew what happened next. After entering the country, they began to break doors to steal everything they could find in those houses. Those who resisted, those who refused to deliver the money or jewels was slaughtered without pity. This way Michele Petrone was killed and afterwards his wife was killed, as well; they refused to deliver the hidden money to Ninco Nanco. An eighty-year-old man, named Sassano, found in bed because of his illness was burned alive after having been rolled into the mattress covered with petrol. The notary Guarino, a wealthy and cultured man, had been taken hostage in the hope of obtaining a large reward; but while he was accompanied on the streets, was killed by a stranger with two gunshots.

This murder, which was laid on me, was actually made by one of the victim's countrymen who had joined our band in the city and wanted to avenge with those gunshots many vexations received .

The country was destroyed; I saw with my own eyes the palace of a certain Maggio, the rich owner of the place, falling in ruins; the brothers Brindisi's buildings, that belonging to Sassano and twenty more that I cannot remember at the moment were devastated.

I stayed at the mayor's place, in the best palace remained unscathed in so much destruction and there I witnessed many acts of barbarism committed by my robbers eager for fury and blood. As for me, I devoted myself to collect ducats, imposing sizes to the richest men of the area, threatening them to kill them or burn their houses.

The massacres and slaughters in Trivigno mark a sad page in the history of my life; Borgjes, correctly put the blame on me, but he did not realize that if the massacres and the looting had not been done, my band would not have helped him.

My men were tired because of the long marches carried out, tired of an inactivity and a rigor opposite to their habits of free life; passing respectfully near some towns, they were badly resigned, their hope of having a rich prey, every kind of pleasure, a deserved wage had been vanished, and I had been barely able to restrain them from accomplishing acts of rebellion; if I had tried to save Trivigno, my band, already discontented, would have perhaps rebelled against me, as well.

On the 5th of November, my band occupied without a shot the small village of Calciano on the right side of the river Basento when brutal acts without regard to people and properties were multiplying.

On the public street I run into a woman brutally murdered and see a thick smoke rising all around, because of those settlers' miserable places set on fire after the looting. The country is poor, so I sometimes impose rewards and collect money.

From Calciano the soldiers marched towards Garaguso, made of another small group of houses on the left of the stream Salandrella. At half way we were received by the priest, who blessed us begging for mercy and protection for his faithful. The country is spared, some little riots happen because of the brutality of some of my men, but they are nothing compared to the massacres of Trivigno and the destruction of Calciano.

The morning after the occupation of Garaguso, Salandra is attacked. The country is barricaded; the Mobile Guard and the National Guard with 200 guns have occupied the feudal castle and from the top of their little fortress show a valuable strength. Some of our men are dead, several others are injured, including my servant, a very reliable person; but the populace is hostile to the lords and murmurs and threatens a lot. The passage is opened and we enter the city, destroying and devastating. The defenders of the castle are our prisoners, someone is beaten up, someone else is killed, most of them are safe. The looting and the fire last all night long; the dead are many, someone is found charred through the steamy ruins.

Leaving Salandra we headed for Craco where we met half way a procession of women and children led by the priest with his cross. They came to ask for clemency for their country and this clemency was given to them, as just small disturbances difficult to avoid with so many people, actually with people with that kind of nature, happened. From Craco after having crossed the river Agri we arrived in Aliano.

When I arrived, this town of about 4000 inhabitants was almost deserted, as the lords and the middle-class had all fled towards Corleto, Perticara and Stigliano, leaving just the rabble in the country. I was received well enough by those miserable people; I stationed in the palace of a gentleman, who had fled with his family to Montalbano Jonico, where I was treated like a real sovereign by the factor and his men. And I began to consider myself a master, and I said to myself that after all I would have been satisfied with that little dukedom, as long as I was left in peace and I was considered a lord and a master who could collect the fruits of his lands. In a sudden, the Sub-Prefect of Matera arrived to disturb my thoughts. He was jealous of my happiness and had collected 1,200 men among a battalion of infantry, of riflemen and of the National Guard, and putting them in two columns, crossing converging roads, he had directed them against me.

It was morning and I was having breakfast when the captain of the guard arrived and with a playful tone said, "Duke of Aliano, we have within our reach a fair strength; it began in Stigliano and is directed against us; our informers who accompanied you, say that 1200 men, divided in two columns and led by a major, have left Matera. The soldiers who come from Stigliano (3 companies of the 62nd infantry and a battalion of the mobile guard), according to what our spies said, are very tired because of the long trip from Matera to here."

I ordered the captain to gather the whole group and to wait for me at the exit of the country; I greeted the maid, a nice and very polite lady with brown hair, said goodbye to the farmer and asked him to thank in my name the distant lord, I picked up my arms and with great regret I left my little palace.

Meanwhile the troops had descended into the plain of the Taverna dell'Acinello and was about to cross the river Sauro, lacking of waters. I asked the leaders for their opinion and their advice to attack the troop on the river was unanimous, while the knights with wide lateral movements at the right time had to assault the Mobile Guard.

Given the necessary orders and taken the appropriate measures, we went down to the plain walking indoor along paths coasted by thick hedges; arrived at the river bed, we stationed opening the fire very quickly.

The troop had occupied a strong position consisting of a small wooded knoll almost close to the stream, near the mill Acinello; they, staying behind the thick poplars, opened a furious fire against us, and several of the gang had already fallen killed. Our great superiority in number was barely able to fight against those damn men from Piedmont, who when the valuable captain gave instructions alternated the fire with continuous attacks. Since I saw my knights who were about to surround my position, I decided to move forward attacking.

I did not have the time to do it, as for fear of being encircled, the two companies of the 62nd Infantry, who threatened us more closely, retreated fighting and took their position at the foot of a hill.

In the meanwhile my soldiers, after a great fire, were advancing jolting along and running. I told Ninco-Nanco, who commanded the knights, to go indoors, on the edge of the forest, in order to go to the side of the troops, in case of an attack to the bayonet.

The maximum fear of the men of my band, and what was creating in me a strong concern for the outcome of the struggle, were the attacks to the bayonet. That full contact fight against people who did not know what a danger was and advanced in spite of our intrepid shooting, with their bayonets, when the word "Savoia" was shouted, made also the strongest soldiers, already hardened to harsh trials, feel a thrill in their veins.

The moving militia going to the right towards Stigliano, was for a moment unprotected on its lateral part; the smart-Ninco Nanco seized the moment and with his 100 men suddenly assaulted the column, causing confusion at first and afterwards fear which provoked a cluttered escape.

The victory was certain for us, especially as the Mobile militia by fleeing had dragged a lot of drifters of the 62nd infantry's companies. It was right that those two companies paid a high price for their audacity, they dared to feel superior to more than a thousand of us, and so I ordered that they could not find a way of retreating.

The commander, I think his name was Pellizza, animated his good men from Piedmont with his words and his example, and, armed with a rifle as a normal soldier, continued to fire against us, without considering our encirclement. While the struggle was going on, one of my soldiers, crawling on the ground, succeeded in advancing near the enemy position, and with a perfect shot, hit the face of the brave officer, who fell dead on the spot.

At this sight, the few survivors fired the last cartridges and afterwards, when they realized to be threatened from all sides, gathered all together and with a desperate assault arrived at my soldiers' position, managing to save themselves, not being chased, heading for Stigliano .

The triumph was complete for us, so that we remained masters of the field and of the many rifles of the dead, and of those rifles thrown away by the soldiers of the confused mobile guard.

When I arrived near the dead captain, I saw that they had already torn his head off the body. My soldiers blamed a Hungarian soldier taken prisoner, and they attributed the reason of that episode to the hope to save his life by performing a true brigand's action; perhaps the head of the respectable captain Pellizza was torn off by my companions, to make a tribute to the murderer; anyway, in order to prevent another massacre on the body of a hero, died away from his country, and subordinated to his King, Börjes imposed and managed to get that the corpse and his objects were delivered to the nearby convent of Stigliano, so that the Prefectural Authority behaved as it wanted to.

The citizens from Stigliano were prepared to welcome the army as they considered them as the savior of their country; they were waiting for them at the entrance of the city to accompany them into the city, but the first soldiers of the Mobile Guard arrived talking about their defeat. The news, that we, about two thousand men, had won beyond Taverna Capo Rotondo, made those poor people abandon every desire to celebrate, every thought of fighting, and while the troops continued their retreat on St. Mauro Forte, after stealing everything they could (money, jewelry, clothes), they moved on the street that arrives at St.Mauro with their wives and their children under the troop's protection.

This considerable mass of people (in Stigliano there were only the poor) was walking on that dusty road and I would say that they were the first, as behind them there were the soldiers of the Mobile Guard and finally the survivors of the 62nd infantry, as a protection against the extreme audacity of the brigands.

My name had to be well-known in those countries and more than the name, my deeds were. I was called the general of a band of two thousand armed men, among those there were 300 knights who frightened the population. The exaggerated statements of the ferocious acts we made raised that fear. I do not deny that Coppa, Ninco Nanco and Caruso sometimes committed ferocious acts on the wounded, and some others disfigured the corpses of the dead, but I assure that I helped some men, and it is not true that when we caught a burgeois, an officer or a soldier, then we had to kill them.

I was the master of a country and I imposed on the rich large rewards that were essential for my men's survival, nor I demanded more; in addition, I did not have such an authority over my numerous companions that I could impose on them the respect for the property and the family, so more than once it happened that after the lords had given me half of their possessions, they had to give the other half to their lieutenants, and see their men been raped without being able to react, otherwise they would have been killed. This was the true reason why we were considered as God's scourges, and was the only reason why the lords of Stigliano were forced to escape to survive. All those people were walking, as I said, on the road that from Stigliano leads to St. Mauro, protected by the troops, when suddenly they unexpectedly met my 100 knights who were coming back to the country after a long period of exploration.

Those men had been ordered to perform a broad movement to the left of Gorgoglione to suddenly attack the position occupied by the troops, and to make sure that the other column, left from

Matera and stationed in Tricarico for some days, had not reached such a position that they could immediately help the troops defeated by me.

Therefore, the meeting was entirely fortuitous; my men seeing those people fleeing began to loot, but when they noticed the presence of the troop ran away returning to the place of our bivouac.

Caruso, who was in charge of that detachment, told me the touching scene of that unpredictable encounter. When the first knight of the band appeared, all those people, who fled frightened to save themselves from that imminent danger, believed they were lost, so emanating cries and lamentations, relied on the Mobile Guard. And as the road was not large and at that point was situated between the mountain and the sea, a large part of people fell into a ravine below, while the others fled, crying, towards the open countryside. And among those three thousand people, we could see the nurse breastfeeding a baby, followed by a fearful lady, worried about the fate of his little born baby, and some faithful servants who were barely dragging their old masters who were unable to move because of the fear and the thrill. Some families were encircled by their fully armed guardians and under the protection of these trusted people they were waiting for the end of the tragedy, sure that his defenders would have let themselves be slaughtered before surrendering. There were even the gentlemen who were alone to defend themselves, because of the iniquities committed against the people, as well as shameful abuses, greed, arrogance, violence of every kind, always unpunished, always tolerated. Even today it is said that the reaction was the result of ignorance, this will be true, indeed it is really true, but in order to promote the reaction there were also these angry lords of the province, who, with insolent boastfulness said, "Our time has arrived". And the poor outraged men said: "Our time has arrived, as well," and so in many countries there were killings, assassinations, predations; the fruits of the civil war.

I was received in Stigliano by the priest, a fat priest, dressed for special occasions, that came up to me and offering me the crucifix to kiss, invoked the compassion and mercy for his followers remained in the country. There was in me and in my band members a sense of religion that made us fearful of God; each of us had the sacred Virgin image, which gave us the strength to survive in spite of the conflicts, so the prayer of the priest and the view of the Crucifix, exerted on me and on my band a strong influence.

The priest's serious words affected my soul so much that I ordered that the prisoners were immediately released by giving them two hours to leave the country. I ordered my men with an unusual insistence, the utmost respect for people, giving severe punishments to those who disobeyed, and so, after reassuring the clergy, I was prepared to enter the country. I got the invitation to occupy the palace by Prince Colonna, and I headed for the accommodation said to me, when the priest invoked my clemency to forty prisoners locked up in a prison. I soon ordered that the prison's doors were opened and freedom was given to each one of them, regardless of the crime or the offense committed.

My band had lavish accommodations, as well, and as all the palaces of the lords were empty, the centurions stationed there. Arriving at Palace Colonna, a truly royal house (when there was the vassalage, the Colonna family ruled the whole country), I was received as a respectable person was usually received. And at that time I was considered as someone important, because after all in this world it was necessary to have the strength to kill people in order to be considered respectable.

Napoleon I was the son of a poor clerk, and by slaughtering millions of men, including my uncle Martino, became a great man, but finally, because he wanted too much, lost everything, and, like me, ended his life in prison, he was in St. Helena, controlled by the British soldiers, and I was in St. Stefano's bathroom, under the strict vigilance of the Italian army's sentinels.

I'd be content with the lordship of that village of Aliano, but I have to die in the penitentiary! But patience, I will die blessing, thanking the clemency of King Vittorio Emanuele, who did not let me die and turned my punishment into hard labors. I thank him, not because I could live longer, but because he let my relatives get rid of the humiliation to hear "You are the grandchildren of a hanged man."

In my real home, accustomed to the rough life of the fields, I was not uncomfortable, and soon learned to adapt to the needs of the noble life. In the evening in that dining room, where who knows how many barons, counts, dukes, marquises, and maybe some kings had dined, I had dinner, too. The table was sumptuous, the servants were gallant; I had the first place, then about thirty people sat down at that table. The servants elegantly dressed, were subordinated to my actions.

The comings and goings of the dishes, each of them extremely refined, had been lasting for about half an hour, and I had not tasted the food, yet, while my officers soon devouring everything appreciated the refined food, obviously not prepared for us but for the dead captain and his soldiers. Shortly after my faithful servant (God rest him in peace as later he died for me), gave me some bread, some cheese, two apples, some nuts and five hard-boiled eggs, and this was my lunch for that hard day.

The night before, in the same dining room a long meeting on us between the killed captain and the aristocracy of the country had been held. And at the table there had been a toast to my capture and that of Börjes; but the captain Pellizza (since I was told) the evening before his death was in a gloomy mood and seemed to have presaged his end, because he repeated several times:

"I will be alive in their hands, I will die as it is right to." In the morning, perhaps impressed by the number of soldiers under his command, with whom he had to fight against more numerous forces, the brave captain, having considered all his serious responsibility, had become sad and pensive, and while pretending to be happy, talked to their men about their certain death. Maybe in the soul of the valiant man, with the arrival of the critical moment, there was not the hope of being helped by the Mobile Guard anymore. Maybe an inward presentiment warned him that in his final hour, it would have been left alone with hid Piedmont men to fight against twenty people; however, when his hosts told him "goodbye", he answered with parting words.

After lunch everyone went where they wanted and I was accompanied to my bedroom.

That night I could not sleep, I walked, I thought, I thought again, but my conscience was bothering me, I saw before my eyes the killed captain, the massacred and mutilated soldiers; I heard the cry of the dying against whom my companions had inveighed to make their deaths rougher; one by one they showed themselves before my eyes, what terrible ghosts, thousands and thousands of men fallen in the past fights, and sparks of fire came out from their empty eyes, while they addressed a lot of curses to me. Shaken, too nervous, I sat on my bed. My head was like a volcano; my throat was burning, my wrists were heavily palpitating, it seemed that my heart wanted to come out of my chest. But a thought immediately arrived to relieve my dejected spirit and someone came to comfort my conscience: my mother!

"And who cries for your poor mother died at the hospital of the insane? And who pays attention to your begging? I said to myself;

who takes pity on your slavery? Perhaps the gentleman that agreed agreed you to work for him with a pay of two francs a month and a loaf of black bread to fill my stomach does?! Was it charity working night and day, during the storms, the rains, during the cold days, the difficult winter, and under the command of the strict castaldos? It would have been charity if you had received so much bread as that your master gave to his dogs; if they had spent for you, for your physical and moral well-being, the thousandth part of what was spent to feed those dogs. But instead you were exploited, and the fruit of your labor was used by your masters as a diversion. If you had continued your uncle Martino's school, you would not have become a ferocious and wild man and maybe you would have been a good father, an honest citizen ... but ...".

I was thinking about these things, when the predatory trumpet rang as it was morning.

I got up in a good mood; half an hour later the captain in service informed me that everything was proceeding normally. Börjes had ordered that the cavalry at dawn controlled the surrounding area up to a distance of six miles at least, gathering news above everything being out of the ordinary, and that they informed him of that.

Alone in my princely palace, I began to walk in the splendid rooms, stopping in the so-called gallery of paintings. Looking here and there a magnificent painting of the beginning of a battle attracted me. The archers were doing skirmishes, the slingers were throwing stones, the pedestrians with a lance and a pike were resting and the knights with their lowered weapons were ready for the endeavour. Among all there was a noble knight, depicted with a larger size compared to the others who were fighting. He was on a horse covered with iron and his shining cuirass was covered with iron, as well; he had in his right hand a huge sword, representing his role as a commander; he had a solemn appearance and was staring at the beginning of the fight.

I do not know how much true he was, but I thought that the knight should be someone belonging to the family Colonna di Stigliano, so I began to speak with him as he was a real person and said: "Sir, your demeanor told me that you are accustomed to the art of the war, that you are brave and you are not afraid of dying. Are you more valiant than me? I bet that if you were in Stigliano yesterday, you would have run away like all the others, in spite of the huge sword you keep in your right hand. Do you want to be braver than the captain Pellizza who died shouting "Long live to the King"? Well, do you want to know who killed that hero? A sixteen-year old boy who taking advantage of his quickness, slipping from bush to bush, arrived cautious and unnoticed at thirty meters far from him, and shot him with a half ounce bullet.

"Your virtuous ancestors, who were knights like you, by fighting have given you the virtue of being able to lead people to the slaughter, and now you cultivate those virtues; you are a prince, a lord, you have been depicted on this painting to commemorate your lineage, do you want more?

"But for me, a poor child of misery, who will be the painter who will paint my entry into Stigliano? No one, as no one cares of a plebeian thief? So, it is over!

"Let's finish it, we do not have to think about the world's infamy, as it is precisely because of D. Vincenzo C.'s infamy that I will disturb the arrogant and noble lords' houses as long as I can."

In Stigliano we stopped for two days, on the 10th and the 11th of November. All the lords had run away, so we decided to continue our march. In addition, Börjes had the strong desire to arrive soon at Potenza. And here we are in the poor village of Cirigliano where we find a few rifles to arm the new recruits, as well as good pigs and a fine wine for our table. After dinner and paid the band, we left to go to Gorgoglione where we managed to conquer the village without shooting. The spies tell us that crossing the valley of Angri, a strong column of soldiers is advancing towards us. The events of Stigliano had strongly impressed not only the people but even the government. The prefects, the sub-prefects, the royal commissioners wanted the Ministry to give them numerous reinforcements of troops ready to fight against the invasion, while the liberals who were bolder and braver by encouraging the timid and the fearful were gathering the national militia crossing the small villages and the biggest towns. From St. Arcangelo, from Montemurro throughout the valley of Angri the soldiers had gathered and had created an enveloping movement with the regular troops, sure that they would have attacked us in a sudden, without letting us escape. A meeting among the leaders is held and the prevailing idea is to avoid the fight venturing into the woods of the mountain.

Familiar with that place and accustomed to the live in the bush, it was not difficult to us to avoid the war plan of the troops' commander, and while he believed that he would have found us at Guardia Perticara, on the 13th we were in Accettura, Oliveto and Garaguso, stationed in this last country. On the 14th our column stationed in Grassano and held out against an attack by the regular troops. After a lively gunshot between our outposts and the soldiers who were following us, in the evening, the troops, having only a little strength, remained there, and before dawn along the bed of a dry stream, we arrived, not being chased, at S. Chirico, which was occupied without a shot.

We attacked Vaglio six miles far from Potenza that held out against our attack with admirable value. If you do not give up, the threat of destruction increases the citizens' desire to protect their place; our MPs are greeted with gunfire; we have several deaths. Divided into four columns we simultaneously attack four parts, and occupy the country while in the convent, strongly occupied, the opposition goes on. Our men, enraged by the unexpected defense, kill everyone they meet on the way, men and women, and set fire to the convent.

The country is ransacked, people steal as much as possible. We leave the convent burning. On the 16th of November we are in the valley of Potenza to release the political prisoners confined there. We are confident that when we arrive there will be a general insurrection. In each of us there is the strong hope of a rich booty and many pleasures. The secret and reactionary committee is chaired by Mr... a former country leader in 1860, a tricolor flag's liberal, who did not manage to become rich in the revolution, because the triumvirate Albini, Boldoni, Mignogna had provided him with everything, changed his favorite flag and became Bourbon, as he was before 1860. But unfortunately this political chameleon once again changed flag, warned the commander La Piazza, pointed at the place where the weapons secretly received just before, were laid, pocketed the Bourbon ducats, and then was proud of having saved Basilicata. In order not to expose him, he killed on the square of St. Gerardo di Potenza (November 1861) five people, the same people who had been ordered to keep the weapons sent from Naples. With my pain I had to abandon the enterprise of subduing Potenza and go back with my tails between my legs like a humiliated dog. We fall back on Pietragalla where we arrive when it is getting dark and we are greeted with gunfire. The Mobile Guard closes themselves into the ducal castle and throughout the day after, hold out against our vigorous attacks. We have many wounded men and some dead soldiers but we are compensated for that by a rich booty. The country is in flames; the militias from Acerenza and Forenza arrive to protect the citizens and we are forced to abandon the enterprise.

The intense cold arrives, the persistent rains cause many diseases, my soldiers are ill and unable to continue the fight. Börjes is in danger of being killed by his robbers. In Avigliano there are armed people and we are rejected. The dissolution makes its way among us, the French commander wants to impose his ideas on Börjes', the civil war in the band is imminent. On the 22nd of November we attack Bella, a small town not far from Ruvo del Monte.

I left at night at the head of my companions and I arrived at dawn at the entrance of the country, where I let my band rest for a while. As happened in Ruvo I sent a letter to the Mayor and ordered them the payment of a reward and the provisioning for my men and horses. I was answered with the sound of the bells, which was a signal of alarm and defense. I accepted the challenge, and after nine hours of fierce fighting I managed to force the armed citizens to enter the feudal castle, which was not possible to conquer. As the master of the country, half in flames, I seized oxes, goats and everything I could and afterwards retired on the mountains unmolested.

We leave the mountains and approach Muro Lucano, that is well protected, as we are informed by some confidants. The French man is not brave enough to attack, because he is afraid of the wrong way; we descend along Platano and arrive at Balvano welcomed by those common people who give us everything.

From Balvano we arrive at Ricigliano where we are greeted with music and with a gathering of priests. The country is looted, the frightened gentlemen give us hospitality and are robbed, those who complain are killed.

The first snow falls on the mountains, winter is arriving, there are a lot of desertions among us, the band is obviously tired and wants to go back to their old profession, without caring of political brigandage anymore. We come back to Basilicata and attack Pescopagano which we are able to occupy looting, destroying and burning after a fierce fighting. The spies warn us that numerous columns of regular troops are approaching us, so we leave the country, chased by the country soldiers who had held out in the reinforced baronial mansion.

In order to avoid the encirclement, we head for the mountains dividing us into groups; the meeting place is the above castle in the Monticchio forest.

Börjes is finally paid off, he leaves with his Spaniards and with very few faithful men, about thirty. His departure does not move us, in fact we caused it as we were tired of his command. I get rid of superfluous elements, promising them to meet in the following spring.

CHAPTER SIX - ISOLATED ATTACKS

I come back to the Toppacivita brush, the field of my victory. But strangely, it was gone! All that remained was the moved soil. The general Della Chiesa with three battalions of riflemen and artillery and cavalry had arrived in Rionero. At the Toppacivita brush, during my absence, there had been a band of eighty bandits led by Pio Masiello; he had maintained the position and the thrill in the district because of the lack of soldiers. The general with his force at first attacked the position with the artillery; at the grenades' explosion the robbers escaped, those who were not killed, fell prisoners and then the band was destroyed. The general after realizing that that position in the hands of bold and numerous robbers was a great danger to Rionero and the neighboring countries, ordered that it was destroyed. With a public announcement he allowed the farmers to cut the wood in that spot, and so very quickly the brush of Mr. Filippo Decillo from San Fele became a beautiful smooth field.

We had to look for another district that was not the Toppacivita one. The winter was advancing very quickly, we were 2180 men and 340 horses. We divided into six main fractions, and I founded other twenty small bands of 12 to 20 men; each of these had their own boss, they could bivouac as well as they liked, working on their own to earn their bread, and in case of tracking, they had to return to the main band they belonged. I stationed in the woods of Castiglione, Sassano, Pesco di Razza and Pietra Palumba; all these forests belonged to the town of Calitri, Carbonara, Aquilonia and Monteverde, all countries without troops, controlled by a weak National Guard..

The second band stationed to the right of the river Ofanto inside the Monticchio forest, under the city of Melfi control where there were three companies of the National Guard, sufficient to the service of the cities and the prisons. The third band stationed in the Monticchio forest but not over the river above mentioned, but over the stream of Atella, and had occupied without shooting this country two miles far from there.

The 4th band occupied the Boceto forest, the 5th that of St. Castaldo and the 6th that of Lagopesole.

All these bands were so well spaced that in a few hours they could gather all together; in a few days they built huts, protections, stables, barracks, kitchens and seized the boilers, the barrels, the buckets.

In order to live, there was a forced requisition of oxes, goats, sheeps, we visited the cellars of the neighboring farms to have the wine and the water of the wells or that which fell out of the sky; what paid was the lead.

We were in December and we began to slaughter the pigs, that were very fat because they had grazed in the woods where acorn was abundant. The headquarter was mine, as well as 480 people, 40 horses and over 100 dogs of all breeds, large and almost fierce.

From the first days of December 1861 up to May 5th, 1862, there was nothing that deserved to be reported, since we were not harassed at all. Cities and small towns by command of the Government made the so-called state of siege, forbidding the people to abandon the country; those who disobeyed were killed. So we spent the winter without being disturbed and it was really lucky, because that year there was such a terrible winter that we could not remember one of similar greatness. So much snow had fallen that we could not walk; it made the newspapers say that the robbers were destroyed and starved while we, as brigands, were healthy and strong as many bulls though without the horns.

With the end of winter as the lands had to be worked, it was inevitable to allow the farmers to return to their fields; but a lot of strict rules forbade anyone to carry too much bread and food to their place. It was believed that this way the people would have surrendered because of their hunger and no one knew, or rather pretended not to know, that the gentlemen in order to have less harm from us, had given us the rich farms providing that we "eat, drink but do not destroy." If somebody was reluctant to help us, paid a high price for his refusal and a lot of their wheat fields and their herds of sheeps were destroyed. With the return of the farmers the country regained its normal appearance, and as it had happened in the past, we began again to receive confidences and information. Among many farmers, there were also the spies of the government, but these men were obviously infamous. We met a lot of people, but they were not killed thanks to their profession...

a single well-targeted shot... At the end of March 1862 the districts of St. Angelo dei Lombardi and of Melfi combined their forces to chase us. Alerted by our confidants we prepared to protect ourselves occupying the most dense of the woods.

We were attacked with a live fire by the troops and the national guards but without any result, as we we were favored by the knowledge of those places, managed to escape from the dangerous assaults, revenging on the isolated patrols lost along those thousands of paths full of thick and huge woods.

The pursuit of the robbers, especially in Melfi, was at first feeble and weak, due to the deficiency of regular troops, and this encouraged to multiply the horde of brigands. Our small victories in the fighting against the troops, the great moral and material support received by the reactionaries and the clergy, thrilled us easily, so drunk desirous for blood and ferocity, after unprecedented barbarities, we often considered ourselves as masters of places and times.

However, when the empire of the law began to prevail in the countryside and in the villages, and the people understood the need to accept the laws of the new government, and they touched with their hands the benefits, then the fight against us became alive, insistent and later fierce. After exploiting the countries placed at the foot of the Vulture, as in May 1863 our presence in Monticchio and in the surrounding woods was threatened and poorly safe, we left our usual houses, divided into small bands. Divided into different bands we had also divided the areas within which the bands had to operate, avoiding that each one of them impede the work of the other. Sometimes we established as the meeting place a country of the distant provinces of Bari, Campobasso, Lecce, Foggia, Avellino and so on, and my soldiers, taxing, attacking, imposing rewards and blackmails, traveled along different itineraries, gathering all together in a precise day in a predefined location, make a planned project all united.

But with the raise of the regular forces and with the order of the

National Guards, we had to limit our action restricting its proportions; we could no longer do ferocious attacks against the countries, nor large windings of important centers using a large crowd of knights, but we could only attack the travelers, assault the postal courier, occupy small villages, isolated farms, disappointing with cunning and quick escapes the clashes against the troops, but we had to pay attention not to provoke them when the huge disparity of forces made us confident of an easy victory. There were thousands of partial attacks, I do not remember the exact dates and locations, as in those days I did not take notes, and I could never realize that after 40 years, from the dark prison where I serve my punishment of forced labor in perpetuity, one day I would have written the history of my predatory life. I state, therefore, without a chronological order, everything I remember, putting aside the useless and unnecessary details. I joined Caruso near the woods of Grotta, not far from the village of Serracapriola, when we were surprised at the bivouac by a battalion of the 36th infantry, and after a brave fight we could barely save ourselves inside the bush, leaving several dead among our soldiers and loading our mules with the requisitions made.

While I was retiring in Molise I was informed that a detachment of cavalry from Lucca was occupying an isolated farm; in order to avenge the defeat and lost booty, during the night I decided to surround the farm and to replace the mules left in the wood of Croce with our troops horses.

After placing my gregarious all around I order to surround the farm with the order to attack at dawn. And at the beginning of the day as soon as the first soldiers come out to take care of their personal cleanliness, the first shots of my soldiers, evidence of the attack, begin. Sure of the surprise I order to narrow the encirclement, but I find an unexpected defense; from the numerous windows those brave men assault us with their rifles and reply with derision to my threats to surrender. To save my soldiers, after a large shooting, which lasted for a long time, I order to set fire to the farm using the plentiful straw piled up and numerous bundles of olive branches.

But the fire, the suffocating smoke do not scare those few soldiers who continue to shoot against us, while the trumpet from the top of the observatory, is constantly giving the charged emotion.

The noise of the shots, the signals of the trumpet, the smoke, the flames give the alarm, some spies is running to the country of Rotello to warn the troop, and, when we were about to collect the fruit of our labors, at the cry of "Savoia" we are attacked by a company of the 61st infantry and forced to flee to save our life, leaving behind several dead and a dozen of wounded and prisoners.

One day, it was the middle of October, 1861, at the head of my band I had a fierce battle near the farm Gaudiano in the territory of Lavello, against the 3rd squadron of the Milan lancers, two companies of the 62nd infantry and a company of the mobile guard.

We were in bivouac in the woods waiting for dawn to try an attack against the postal courier, which was carrying a large sum of money to the provincial tax office. It was known that the courier was accompanied by a good crowd of cavalry, but the greed of the rich booty had made us bold and reckless so that we did not realize the risk of fighting against a large armed force.

I was in charge of more than one hundred and fifty soldiers, of whom more than half were on horseback; and the deep and particular knowledge of the location, the precise information of our spies, facilitated our task. The attack at the courier was quick and resolute, but suddenly we found ourselves surrounded by a squadron of cavalry, while from the near fields the infantry and the mobile militia came out running with their bayonets. At the sight of so much force, I ordered to take a position on the high side of the road, safe from the cavalry, and after a large fire to retreat and entern the thickest forest. The attack was a disaster for us, as we left on the ground over forty people dead and wounded.

Eight or ten of our prisoners fell dead, as well, they were killed with the swords, and among them there was the wife of my friend Teschetta, who followed the band dressed as a man.

I remember the sad end of my faithful companion, Volonino's brother, who was killed by a brave sharpshooter of the 11th Battalion.

I was returning from an exploration carried out near the village of Candela, when I was signaled the approach of a detachment of sharpshooters reinforced by a platoon of Hussars. I ordered the retreat and galloping I moved to the opposite side of the Ofanto, entering soon the thick forest. A flanking patrol, commanded by Volonino, suddenly surprised, had no time to escape by using the known ford, and in order not to be attacked by the troop they faced the current in a dangerous point. At this sight the Hussars who were chasing them stopped shooting my soldiers with their guns; unfortunately Volonino's horse after crossing the current approached the shore and began to sink in the mud. As a squirrel, a sharpshooter got undressed and with his rifle began to fight, in spite of the rigorous cold and the waters of the perfidious river, caught the robber, killed him with a terrible shot of bayonet in the chest, and returned to the opposite shore by dragging the horse and the rider.

I traveled with my band the delicious plains of Foggia, the land of Bari, the seashore of Basilicata, I arrived at Lecce, Ginosa, Castellaneta, performing depredations and blackmails everywhere, sometimes escaping from the troops and suddenly attacking, often with an ambush and a trap. Wounded four times, I saw my most faithful soldiers one by one my falling dead, some of my beloved companions abandoned me, as they preferred the safety of the life imprisonment rather than the death on the field or a shot in their back and at last I was betrayed by a fratricidal Cain, Giuseppe Caruso, but I do not want to hasten the events, I will talk about that at the right time. In June or July of 1862 a part of my band, more than 100 horsemen under the command of Donato Tortora, had been commissioned to attack the postal courier that from San Fele crossing Atella led to Rionero. Secret information had let us know that on that day an office employee of the register of Melfi was traveling with a considerable sum of money, the result of tax collecting made in different countries.

We knew that courier was usually accompanied by a few men of infantry, but thinking that on that day the escort would have been increased, I wanted Tortora to take care of the challenge with a large number of my soldiers, in order not to return empty-handed..

Stationed along the bed of the stream Levata, far from steep banks, my soldiers were ready to go out on the road, near Ponte Vecchio, as soon as the courier had arrived there, sure to scare that corporal, forcing him to flee, as well as a few soldiers who were the escort to the carriage.

And in fact as soon as the courier arrived at the designated point my soldiers killed the driver with a rifle and after surrounding the carriage gathered to collect the money that was stored there, as it had been said.

The escort was walking far from there and on that day it consisted of about forty soldiers of the 62nd infantry commanded by a sergeant. The shotgun, which from a high part had killed the driver, wounded in the face and fallen to the ground, aroused an alarm in the small detachment, which running with their bayonets began to fight.

Greeted with gunfire from my soldiers, the detachment stopped and replied with fire. Later after realizing that they were trying to encircle it, the sergeant ordered to leave the road and went to his position on a small hill near a road of Gaudo, where he began to attack us with a lively fire. The fight lasted for several hours and whenever my soldiers were trying to encourage that group of brave men, they were greeted with the cry of 'Savoia' and forced to load their bayonets.

After two hours, Tortora not having succeeded in scaring the troops, forcing them to flee, as they were afraid of some reinforcements which could arrive from Rionero, turned away and went back to the camp, having left on the scene of the clash twenty brigands killed or seriously injured.

At the end of 1862 with Caruso's band in the woods Grotta in Molise I fought against a company of the 36th infantry reinforced by 100 men of the national guard.

Informed of the column's advancing, thanks to a simulated escape of our soldiers, we attracted the troop in a muddy and bumpy land where we could barely walk. When the company had entered in that kind of morass, we suddenly came out divided into groups and galloping we attacked the soldiers who responded to our fire shooting us surrounded and massacred, no one was able to escape.

The lieutenant, taken alive, was tied to a tree and shot; the captain, later I knew his name was Rota, wounded in the arm by a rifle shot, had the courage to shoot himself in the head. As masters of the field, we undressed and robbed the corpses, the saddest ones, and encouraged by Caruso, performed obscene acts defacing the poor dead; after collecting our dead soldiers and burying them there, we retreated into the thick forest to divide the poor booty. Later numerous reinforcements arrived, and as we had been warned in time we prepared to retire, I decided to change position in search of other

adventures.

I remember as if it were now the terrible battle that took place near Rapolla on a foggy day of November, with a squadron of Saluzzo cavalry.

From the top of St. Paulo, where the band had their camp we were informed that the cavalry from Barile had arrived at Rapolla, they wanted to cross Melfi, reach Spineventola, and from there begin to attack with the encirclement.

Protected by a fairly dense fog, strong thanks to the number and the easy surprise, we decided to attack at the time of the ford.

And the shock was terrible and after a strong struggle we escaped leaving in the bed of the stream a lot of dead and prisoners. That defeat caused the appearance of a feeling of revenge in my spirit and we managed to get a complete and terrible revenge in March 1863 against the same squad. Twenty soldiers led by the lieutenant Bianchi and left from Venosa had arrived at Melfi and after leaving the main road had entered a forest path coasting the shores of a very deep moat.

Our spies had informed us of the departure from Venosa of this tiny platoon and from our hidden position we had followed step by step all their movements, waiting for the right moment to attack.

Stationed in the dense bush, protected by gnarled trees and thick bushes, when the soldiers were quietly advancing by one walking slowly and unarmed, at a precise time and at a given signal a tremendous shot started.

Caught unawares, not very far from there more than half soldiers died, and before they had time to protect themselves, a second group of rifles sounded horribly through the woods, killing the survivors. Those who did not die because of the rifles were slaughtered with a knife or a dagger. The lieutenant and sergeant were still alive,and thanks to the work of Teodoro, were found with their heads divided from their bodies, that were nailed to a tree with the words "The fallen in Rapolla have been avenged."

On that day Tortora and Teodoro committed acts of savage barbarity towards the fallen soldiers, nor I could impose my will not to ruin those bodies, as, slightly wounded by a shot of guns, I had to stay inside the wood to treat my small but painful wound. And as I recalled the clashes I had against the cavalry I cannot but talk about the miserable end of another platoon of cavalry under the command of Lieutenant Borromeo.

We were in July; in a sweltering evening after a very hot day, we were informed of the arrival at Melfi of a platoon of cavalry; the ambush was decided: Tortora, Caruso, Theodore with their bands, had to prepare the trap, and after choosing a dense hedge that bordered the road as their position, their men stationed there, while about other twelve men on their horses were inside the backyard of a farmhouse.

When the troop, unconscious of the trap, parading along the dusty road arrived near the position, the robbers opened the fire and with repeated discharges killed the bold knights, while the other bandits on horseback, after leaving their hiding place, killed with the knife and guns those who were simply injured. The lieutenant, alive by a miracle, had to thank the speed of his superb horse for his survival. Chased up to the walls of Venosa, he could barely save from the strenuous pursuit Teodoro, and from a hundred strokes shot at his back.

I am sorry to be unable to write in detail all the episodes of my life as a brigand in the years 1862, '63 and '64. I remember that our bands were the terror and despair of Puglia, Basilicata and Campania. There the cavalry, the infantry, the riflemen, the Hungarian mobile guards set on us could not defeat us. How many calls I had from the generals, the prefects, the great lords who wanted me to surrender, but I was more afraid of prison, even still alive, rather than a death in a battle.

In the forest of Lagopesole an captain of the 13th infantry, the delegate of Avigliano and a sergeant had the courage to approach us without carrying their weapons to encourage us to surrender with the promise that we would not have been killed. I refused and ordered Ninco Nanco to accompany those brave parliamentarians out of the woods without killing them.

I learned afterwards that Ninco Nanco, far from me, had killed those three valiant men ordering his men to keep the secret.

Only once I thought about going unarmed to my enemies in order to put an end to my life as a brigand, and without wasting time, accompanied by Tortora and Ninco Nanco, I advanced helpless toward Rionero. The person sent to me by the commander La Piazza to discuss the terms of my surrender, listened to my pretensions asking for a safe-conduct and a truce.

But even before he could answer I had changed my mind, and I had gone back to my arms and my safe woods of Monticchio, more courageous than before to sell my life and freedom at a high price. To many people it may seem weird that my band, so numerous and formidable, was able to domineer from 1861 to 1864 and that in spite of the relentless pursuit of the troop, I was able to cross unharmed the territory that divides Basilicata from

Rome.

The lords with their powerful aid, or at least with their silence, contributed for the most part to our salvation. A I wrote, during the various years of my life as a bandit, I slept a few times at the bivouac, and I found a place to rest and something to eat thanks to people all considered intangibles in every respect. I was never betrayed; many of these people did not betray me even though threatened them for fear, and others gave me shelter for profit and others for greed.

I'm still a creditor of several thousands of ducats lent to a reverend priest, who then escaped to Naples when I asked him for a refund.

Another factor that contributed so much to our salvation was the espionage. Our confidants were at the same time informants of the government and then salaried by the State, therefore we were almost always aware of the troops' movements; and more than once, in order to give merit and prestige to our confidants (who were at the same time our and the government's confidants) we ourselves sent very accurate information to the Command Zone about place of our bivouac. And when the troops arrived at the place to chase us, as we had time to realize their strength, we attacked them or we flee in time, according to our interest.

A lot of confidants were part of the National Guard and thanks to them there were sometimes accurate information about the place where the weapons were stored, about the location where the night patrols were normally stationed, so we often proceeded without failing.

Our vast knowledge of the country, the predominantly wooded terrain, theater of our gestures, the acquired habit of having a wild life, sometimes forced to beg for the daily bread, forced to wander greenhouse by greenhouse through thorn bushes, through deep moats, a really hard sobriety, were powerful factors that helped to make us strong and feared.

Due to the fairly large number of the bands' components and even more to the brutality of many of us, we were often found hated by the populace, from which we were all out; but in general it often helped us in all our businesses. This help, almost always spontaneous, was the result of the populace's innate hatred against the royal officials and the soldiers from Piedmont, because of the effects of the Pica law, and the contemptuous manner with which the officers used to treat the populations, considering them all the same. Before 1861, when Franceschiello reigned in Naples, a lot of soldiers belonging to my band came from the cops' oppressions committed by Del Carretto's men, by people who did not want to surrender before absurd oppressions, two did not want to sell the honor of their wives or daughters to young and arrogant squires, so they were persecuted, considered criminals, vagrants, people who easily committed crimes.

After the government of Vittorio Emanuele a lot of men persecuted by the so-called group of counter-reactionaries (with bossing swagger, under the law's protection, they committed crimes which were not inferior to the robbers' ones and with low and cowardly revenges denounced masters and servants to the police to get rid of their personal enemies) increased the number of our soldiers.

Among their whims, those who got benefits were we who recruited people who influenced the poor a lot.

Among the various bands that were stationed in Basilicata, I can say without fear of being contradicted that mine was the most orderly and the best organized. Coppa, Ninco Nanco, Caruso, Tortora, Serravalle and many others who were in charge of bands, were all my employees, and they always felt a feeling of respect for their general.

My gregarious men loved and obeyed me without the need for coercive measures, I was sometimes forced by the needs of the moment to give some severe examples in order to regulate the hordes, but I was always reliable and friendly with everyone, rather than commander. All my desire was orders to my soldiers and in some risky operations, where a few bandits had to fight, it was painful to me to always reject the spontaneous cooperation of my companions who voluntarily offered themselves for the enterprise. I had calls from Generals and Prefects where they promised me not the freedom, because it would not be true, but an insurance of life, if I would have met them; I always rejected every invitation, convinced that I would be locked in a prison forever, since I was the general captain of all the brigands of Basilicata. Many of my followers lured by the hope of a mild sentence, without informing me, met the general Fointana in Rionero and they received not serious convictions, compared with the crimes committed. They were always hated by me and considered cowards every day.

CHAPTER SEVEN – THE ESCAPE AND THE IMPRISONMENT

Among the cowards who abandoned us to meet the Authority, the basest was certainly Giuseppe Caruso. This wicked Cain, after having committed fratricidal crimes arrived there with his evil companions, and after a few months was released by the Government. So at the head of the troop he began to look for his companions, and within a few months gave the government a service that he had never given to the powerful army.

Caruso, the vile murderer of Pio Masiello, contributed to the killing of his unique brother, and that blood still wants revenge against him, now free and a royal employee, after having killed 124 men, during the four years of his career as a bandit.

But things had to happen this way; the holy words of the priest Leonardo Cecere had to come true, "the sad kill the sad" but that vile mercenary, that sold soul, did not have the pleasure of seeing me caught because of his work, and ha has to thank the infamous Roman Curia, if he had the fortune to attend, as a free citizen, to my death sentence. God is right, and when I will go to the other world I will treat him as Ugolino treated the Archbishop Ruggeri. Caruso after becoming the advisor of the general Pallavicini explained how a predatory war had to be done; he perfectly knew our innermost shelters, our habits, our confidants, our soldiers, so at the head of the troop he contributed to our dissolution.

It was on his advice that the so-called military posts placed at the outlets and in the streets between one forest and the other were established, and it was because of him that we were then attached in our safe hiding places by his troops. But his sagacity, his great cunning, the bitterness of his black soul were unable to influence me, in fact I could always escape from his relentless pursuit. One day he encircles the cave where I am but that naïve man does not remember that the cave has two ways out and while he wants me to die, feels that I am already safe on the summit of the mountain that has his name. Dejected, derelict, he follows me with his men up to the mountain Caruso where he attacks us with the fire of their rifled guns, and when he is sure of having killed me and wants to pick up my body as a sign of victory, he realizes, but too late, that the dead man is not me, but my servant wearing my general clothes. And so on I escape from him on the Ofanto when he is in charge of thousands of soldiers and arrived safe in then Sassano woods, he so stunned by my boldness and luck that he cannot understand the reason why he was unable to catch me. We are at the end of June 1864, we are twelve friends who are contemplating sad and grieved the dead body of our proud comrade Pio Masiello. He lies dead on the edge of a moat; his eyes are lifeless, his lips are livid, his teeth are clutched and his hands are straight. His chest is lacerated by several deep dagger wounds. At his feet there is his discharged rifle. Caruso triumphs. Ninco Nanco, Masiello, Rocco Serra, Grippo, La Rocca are dead, the others are prisoners, all that remains is death or jail! My legion of brave and audacious companions had thinned tremendously. At the beginning my soldiers were two thousand but in 1864 there were just one hundred and sixteen men, all wounded from two to five times. Eighty-six soldiers had fallen alive into the hands of the force, sixteen men had been shot, a hundred and twenty had spontaneously surrendered, the others had all died with their weapons in their hands.

I realized, with deep sorrow, that my star was close to sunset; the threatening shadow of Caruso began to make me feel thoughtful; Melfi, that had been the scene of the fight and a strong fortress of the strenuous pursuit, had become an unsafe place to me; I could see in every person, also in my companions, a traitor, a coward man able to sell my person in order to have his sentence mitigated; it must be added to all these events the energetic orders given by the general Pallavicini to accelerate our capture, and it will not be hard to get an idea of my state of mind in those days.

Miraculously escaped from Monte Caruso and the river Ofanto, after having lost the best brothers I could ever have had, I gathered the most faithful soldiers in the forest of Sassano to decide what to do. There were different and various opinions, and among those, the prevailing idea was that of fighting all together against Caruso to avenge our comrade Masiello. On the contrary, because of the difficulty of being all together, without continuously resorting to violence, I informed them that I would have retreated in Rome leaving each one of them free of doing what they wanted.

On the evening of July 28th, 1864 twelve men mounted on superb horses from Puglia, near the town of Monteverde, province of Avellino, challenging for the last time the troop of the Royal Italian Army, then calm and proud cross the national road near the walls of the town of Lacedonoa arriving in the evening near Ariano di Puglia. Those brave knights pass through towns and villages along hidden stretches, the deep woods, the bed of the river, and overcome serious obstacles, face serious dangers, determined to reach the Papal State. Wretched men, where are you going? Who you rely on? What thoughts guide you? Go back to your woods, your brush, go far from the priests' principles as they are viler and more traitors than the ancient Jews!... Of the twelve knights, seven fell sick on the way and tried the law of the government, four other soldiers and I went to Rome. From one of the seven hills I sent to a diplomat from a letter received from a southern lord, who I do not mention so as not to offend his memory. And he answered me, advising me to go to the governor of the Pope, which I did very quickly.

What did the great Pope Pio IX do? He buried us in the new prisons of Rome, and afterwards we were transferred to the prison of San Michele a Ripa always locked in solitary confinement. There was never a reply to my many and repeated entreaties to be delivered to the government of Italy. I asked to have some of my money (seized at the time of the arrest) to eat something else apart from that I was given there, but I was replied by Monsignor Randi Lorenzo, the governor of Rome, "and when you'll be free what will you do if you spend all your money now??'.

The Holy Father after receiving me in his kingdom had to say: "You touched my clothes, you kissed my slipper, your sins are forgiven"; he had to write this way to S.M. Vittorio Emanuele,

King of Italy: "Dearest son. A great sinner arrived here, Carmine Donatelli Crocco. I as the father of Christian children have forgiven his sins so that he will not go to hell forever, and you, my son, as a Christian King, punish him but leave him alive so that in prison he has the opportunity to regain his moral principles and ask God for the forgiveness of the wrong things done on earth, and so with my and your virtue we will send him as a penitent to the final judgment."

But he did not do that way, so I have the right to curse his memory, his three reigns and his villainous curia. Noble children of Italy, you have known and loved King Vittorio Emanuele of the Savoy House. You only need the courage to believe that after the recommendation of the Pope, would I have been executed alike? After 31 months of rigorous imprisonment fed with a pound of bread a day and a vegetable soup, I was sent to France.

Pio IX not to displease the former King, which I had served, and who had advised me to be in Rome saying that I was subordinated to King Giocchino Murat, made the French Embassy give me a passport to Algeria and sent me to France.

I was arrested in France and for three months I enjoyed the delights of a foreign prison plagued by common insects, and by a forced fasting. After the hustle and bustle of diplomatic notes among the courts of Rome, Florence, Paris, on the right of my person, Napoleon III, making every possible effort, from Marseille sent me back to Rome at the disposal of the Pope. After a short time I was sent to the prison of Paliano, where I was unchained and locked in the tower of that fortress, to begin my second fasting, which lasted until September 1870.

Do you know why I was not delivered to the Italian government? Because if they delivered me , they would have delivered also the sum of 19,800 liras I had with me at the time of the arrest, and that amount was not given to me and was not given to the government, as it was right to do, but it ended up in the pockets of some thief lord. Finally, at the end of September 1870 a battalion of the Royal Italian Army arrived at Paliano. Some officers mindful of my deeds, some others who had fought against me in 1861-62, came to visit me in my solitary confinement, and perhaps because of them I had the chains taken off, and I was allowed to go outside.

The general Lanzavecchia took me away from the punishment cell moving me to an other cell spacious and full of light, where I was given a nurse bed, I was fed as a sick people, but at least I ate abundantly, and thereafter I was treated with the respect, that the human goodness usually gives to those wretched men who have to receive a death penalty.

In those days I always cried; I cried not for the fear of death, the only remedy to my pain, but because of the gratitude and I still cry now that I write, for the many mercies I received from those I killed as enemies. I stayed in Paliano until June 23rd, 1871; in the evening of this day I arrived in Caserta. There, a crowd of onlookers was waiting at the train station to admire the famous general of robbers; in prison, waiting to tgo on with my trip, I had the great honor of meeting many lords, moved by the will to know in person, this wild and fierce beast called Crocco.

I went from Caserta to Avellino always escorted and well-treated by the good police.

I stayed locked up in the prisons of Avellino for thirteen months where I underwent continuous questionings by a judge who seemed to me the messiah of the law.

Every day there were two or three big processes, examining one by one the charges, checking the dates, the places and the people. To my regret I left the prison of Avellino and on July 27th, 1872, escorted by a sergeant and four police officers, I arrived in Potenza. There, I did not find curious people, but rather the threatening children of the mob that I had commanded.

The news of my arrival had attracted the sixteen thousand citizens of the town on the streets, apart from St. Gerard everyone was there. To the majority of those citizens' satisfaction, I had already beaten, when we arrived at Porta St. Lucia they made me get off the carriage and walking on the road Pretoriana, I was taken to the police station and from there to the royal court jails awaiting my process. Finally, on August 14th, 1872, a day that I hated most, the halls of the court opened, and some jurors were asked to judge this great offender, who now resigned and humble is writing his story.

The numerous public is barely restrained by the police and a group of soldiers; everyone is curious to see the face of the famous reactionary general of the Melfi brigandage; everyone wants to hear the reading of the long indictment, the enumeration of the hundreds of charges laid against him, the evidence that aggravate the offenses committed, the defense of the accused, the terrible closing speech of the public prosecutor, the mild defense of the lawyers, the impartial summary of the President and, finally, the verdict of the jury.

CHAPTER EIGHT – CONCLUSION

If the reader, curious about examining in depth these pages, wanted to enjoy reading the various parts of my big trial, he would read for a month, as there are a lot of volumes full of documents, which were piled up on the desk of the President the day after my trial.

"The Court" the usher says aloud, and in a sepulchral silence the judges go and sit in their place.

"You, Carmine Donatelli Crocco, son of Francesco and Maria Gerardo from Santo Mauro, born in the town of Rionero in Vulture, in the Melfi district, province of Basilicata, are accused of 75 murders, of those 62 had been truly committed and 13 had been missed, and of one million and two hundred thousand liras of faults, damages, fires, and so on».

The process took place as all processes of this world did and I do not remember the exact minutes, nor remembering them, I will now talk about them, as the exact and detailed description of everything was read and written on that day still exists in the provincial archives of Potenza..

The jurors had no mercy on me, as I had not had mercy on my fellows, the law ran its course and the man who had aroused such terror in Basilicata, who had killed so many people, who had led sorrow in so many families, ended his deeds as a brigand after arriving safe and unharmed in the papal territory:

It is theater for the whole nature

Each one goes on stage

Napoleon with his talent

Died in the island of St. Helena

So Crocco already humble shepherd

Elected general by brigands

After the struggles of blood and terror

Serves in jail the already committed crimes

To assure the reader that in spite of my ferocity, I was generous and kind to those who had never done anything wrong, I beg you to ask Mr. Pasquale Saraceno, one of the richest owners of Atella, honest, liberal and captain of the national guard.

I remember, as if it were now his frank and honest statement made during my process, since he was mentioned as a witness for the trial.

Caught by a patrol of my soldiers led by the fierce Ninco Nanco, the poor Mr. Saraceno was brought before me, so that I established the amount of money he had to give me to be free, and after receiving the money I ordered the kind of punishment he had to take, as captain the National Guard.

Even before he invoke pity for himself, when he was introduced to me, I was sorry for his capture and swore at his naivety that had encouraged him to cross dangerous roads.

I thought of his mother, his lady, I remembered that in the past he had been honest to me, and I swore to myself to release him immediately and at any cost.

I had to fight against the stubbornness of Ninco Nanco and ferocity of Coppa, and as Mr. Saraceno had no money with him, to regain his freedom, I had to be his guarantor, and said if he had not sent 400 ducats, I myself would have paid 200 ducats to Coppa and 200 to Ninco Nanco. And I had the pleasure to see Mr. Saraceno free, in fact I remember that I accompanied him to Atella, to fell surer.

I understand by myself, that many people reading this crude story will fell, and not without reason, a sense of disgust and nausea;

but as it is written that God's mercy is infinite, I hope that even the men's one is infinite, and that after a sincere regret and a 40-year imprisonment, they can redeem the man before the judgment of their fellow man and the sinner before the judgment of God.

With regards to the publishing of my autobiography, it should not be criticized, as this is the original copy written by my hands; so, dear reader, make a wise preface ... I free you from any obligation of respect towards me. Neither I can go under censorship, as the events written by me can be found in the court documents. Those who believed to have been deceived can appeal to the trials recourse to the processes at their own expense and will understand that I am not lying because of boastfulness, that actually for shame I often keep a prudent reserve.

What I really would like to say is that I acted under the impulse of a bigger force, and that if the men had not bombarded me now I would not be famous, but a honest shepherd or farmer, a bit lively and impulsive, maybe a bit overbearing but honest.

I repeat that everything I have written is the pure and simple truth. The story of my poor mother can be clarified in the asylum of Aversa, where the poor miserable woman; in order to analyze in depth my family's events you can write to Rionero where you will find a few survivors who surely remember my father, D. Vincenzo C. ... my sister Rosina, the procuress Rosa, D. Peppino C. killed by me. As for the robbery episodes, I have never exaggerated, if you look at the archives of the municipality devastated by me you will find written me more things than those I have said writing.

The clash of Toppacivita in detail and minutely described by me, as I remember it better than the others because of the victory carried out, can be confirmed by the owner of the forest, Mr. Filippo Decillo from San Fele, who I hope is still alive, even if I have never had anything to do with him.

As for the fight near Molino dell'Aciniello in Stigliano, well remembered by me with minute details, you can write to Mr. Michele Del Monte or, in case of death, to his heirs and you will clearly understand what happened there on the 19th of November 1861.

As for the whole period when I acted with Börjes, there must exist historical memories because the Spaniard continuously took notes that he sent to his commander in Spain. With the decline of robbers the great performances ended, from 1862 to 1864 I do not remember the thousand episodes of my predatory life, so I just mentioned some, the most important and characteristic ones; the others were certainly remembered by some writings of those times, or actually they were written in the official reports that the Commanders and Military Zones sent to the Ministry of the war.

My famous trips along Capitanata, Bari, Lecce, the high Molise, and so on, have left terrible memories, so there will be no country that will not remember cursing them the ravages committed by the well-known band leader Crocco.

So, respectable Mr.... please do not put this writing aside; it is corrected by those who are experts on science and letters, and it will become not delightful, but certainly interesting and worthy to be read. I am sorry for the improper and unbecoming words, the former are due to my lack of culture, the latter are due to my pain, and please correct them so that they do not offend the publishing dignity.

It is not the will to transmit to posterity the memory of the killings made that leads me to ask you to print my writing. Today we read the writings of the past centuries and thanks to the narration of the past events we learn a lot of lessons for the future; in a thousand of years probably these words will be useful, even if now we do not think so. Probably in the future someone, expert on intellectual progress will be born and they will understand what I was looking for, and by reading the history of two thousand and two hundred men all slaughtered in order to let one person survive, they will find an effective remedy to regenerate the human race. I do not think that in this manuscript there is nothing that could encourage people to write about many things.

That poor mutilated man who after being at the service of his country fighting in Iena, in Vienna, in Berezina, returned home without a leg and is forced to take care of sheeps and eat acorns to survive, and therefore being not brave enough to tell his story to the young, advises to be always honest and to be satisfied with the little honestly earned and to reject the much of dubious provenance, offers a vast field of thoughts at the present time.

And I do not think that the fierce bandits' kind idea of burning the corpse of the murdered Pio Masiello and scattering his ashes into the wind, so they could cry revenge against the fratricidal Caruso, should not be ignored.

And finally, it seems useful to me the example of Francesco Attanasio murderer for six times who steals to leave money to the church and the poor, while let the innocent be punished for the crimes he committed.

I have never been able to understand how the social consortium is formed; I know that the dishonest are hated by everyone, all escape from them, the law does not understand them..... and then we call evil those who kill them... and we do not want to understand that everyone is worthy of living.

Printed in Great Britain
by Amazon

Dash Diet: Heart Health, High Blood Pressure, Cholesterol, Hypertension, Wt. Management

Learn How to Lose Weight Fast with Dash Diet Detox, Cleansing Diet, Glycemic Index, Lose 1 Pound Per Week! And Keep It Off!

+ FREE RECIPE BOOK OFFER: **Free Dash Diet Healthy Recipes Offer! with Free Mediterranean Diet Recipes! With** *additional chapter on Simplified Detox!, (includes information about Detox, Cleansing Diet, Glycemic Index, etc.)*

UPDATED ENHANCED EDITION! ADDITIONAL CHAPTERS ADDED!
ISBN-13:978-1494966218

ISBN-10: 1494966212

FREE Bonus Offer: free recipes and other health and wellness related books

Please Click Here for Instant Access to Free Recipe Book
http://www.healthylifenaturally.com/dashdiet/